BREATHLESS

A STORY OF SURVIVAL, HOPE AND HEALING

Staying strong through ARDS, vasculitis, paralysis, and recovery

MARY ANN RODY

ISBN 978-1-63575-474-2 (Paperback)
ISBN 978-1-63575-475-9 (Digital)

Christian Faith Publishing, Inc.
296 Chestnut Street
Meadville, PA 16335
www.christianfaithpublishing.com

Unless otherwise noted, scripture quotations are taken from the Holy Bible, New International Version®, NIV® Copyright © 1973, 1978, 1984, 2011 by Biblica, Inc.® Used by permission. All rights reserved worldwide.

Printed in the United States of America

Dedicated to Jesus Christ, my Lord and Savior,
Who healed and sustained me,
To Him be all the glory, honor, praise
And thanksgiving!

Acknowledgments

Special thanks to my precious family:
My husband, Ryan,
My daughters, Jennifer and Allison,
My son, Michael,
My son-in-law, Alan,
Who lovingly cared for my every need on a daily basis

To my very special and amazing friends,
You know who you are
Who loved me through it all, and
Who gave me their strength, energy, wisdom, and courage

And to those who prayed daily for my healing and recovery,
Thank you from the bottom of my heart,
I love you all forever.

Contents

Preface

Miracles are defined as an event not explicable by natural or scientific laws. In the Gospel of John, miracles are called signs of God's overwhelming power made visible in a remarkable way. Most of us think of miracles as an instant solution, an end to the pain, the heartache, the misery, the problem—whatever it is. Have you ever been in desperate need of a miracle? Those times when the only thing that will help is a direct intervention from God? The pink slip, the foreclosure, the accident, the terminal diagnosis, the betrayal, the loss of a loved one—we have all been there in some way. What can we do to obtain a miracle? An age-old question, for sure, and not many concrete answers! Miracles are something that we wish for, hope for, and pray for. When we feel a need in our lives we often pray, "God, just bring me a miracle!" There is nothing wrong with turning to God at times like these; in fact, He welcomes us whenever and however we turn to him. He is strong when we are weak. He tells us in His word, *"The name of the* LORD *is a strong tower; The righteous run to it and are safe"* (Prov. 18:10). He encourages us to lean on Him as a strong tower, a refuge in time of trouble.

Many remarkable stories tell of people caught suddenly in drastic situations, where only a direct miracle can save them. Their young child falls into a swimming pool and survives, they are in a serious car accident and no one is injured, a friend's house catches on fire but they escape unharmed—the list goes on. Don't we all know someone who survived an accident without a scratch and we have said "It's a miracle!"? Perhaps a student passes a difficult test without ever opening a book, and he exclaims "It's a miracle!" We get the job of our dreams when we were the least likely candidate, and think "It must be a miracle!" When the eyes of our hearts are open, we can see God working in our daily lives.

What about those times when we pray and pray and the answer doesn't come? Although there are times that a miracle comes immediately, often the answer does not come right away. These times can be difficult and confusing. It is easy to allow ourselves to lose hope. We question our faith, and perhaps, we question God. God loves us so much! Those of us with children understand the supernatural, all-consuming love we have for our own children. It has been described by some as "seeing your own heart walking around outside your body!" God tells us in his word that if we love our children *this much*, He loves us as His children even *more*! *"Can a mother forget the baby at her breast and have no compassion on the child she has borne? Though she may forget, I will not forget you!"* (Isa. 49:15) Many parents have said they would give their lives for their children, that they would gladly trade places with a sick, injured, or suffering child. He wants us to hang onto faith and hope even during difficult times.

This is *exactly* what God did for us—He sent His Son, Jesus, to *die for us!* If He loved us enough to sacrifice His Son for us, don't you think that He hears our every prayer and will answer us? He wants to give us every good thing, and promises that He will make this happen. *"And we know that in all things God works for the good of those who love him, who have been called according to His purpose"* (Rom. 8:28). A key phrase to remember in this verse is "according to His purpose." We must always remember that He is sovereign, that He has a plan for our good, that He loves us more than we can imagine, and that He can be trusted.

The Bible tells many stories of miracles happening instantly. But the Bible is also full of stories about ordinary people who asked for God's help and God answered their prayers in His *timing* and in His *way.* Abraham and Sarah waited for decades for a child, and God rewarded them with Isaac, even though Sarah was over ninety and Abraham over one hundred years old! God's timing is often related to His purpose so that when He answers prayer, or when a miracle occurs, God is glorified! God's timing is always perfect. These stories give us and understanding into how God works and help us to have hope. We will look at one such example, Acts 3, which clearly shows God's power and His intention in His miraculous healing. God healed the lame man for all to see, yet the man had been a lame beggar for forty years! The miracle came in God's time, and many thousands were affected.

God rewards and honors faith, trust, and perseverance. In the process of praying and then waiting in expectation for God's answer, we deepen our knowledge and our relationship with the Almighty, and in that process, God's purposes are revealed and achieved. Waiting time is full of opportunities to learn about ourselves, about God, and about our relationship with God. What God wants more than anything is to have a *deep* relationship with us, and the more time we spend in praying, the closer we become to Him. We will find the answers we are seeking if we keep praying in faith and trust. *"But seek first his kingdom and his righteousness, and all these things will be given to you as well"* (Matt. 6:33). God is always faithful, and the answer will come in time, but we must be faithful as well.

God is the one in control, and although He cooperates with us by answering our prayers and meeting our needs in His way and in His time, He is also our sovereign Lord and Savior who has spoken the universe into existence. He is the Alpha and the Omega, the first and the last; He sees all of time into eternity and knows what is best for us in every situation. Although He has blessed us with the gift of our free will, He is also weaving our lives together into a glorious tapestry, which we will only be able to view when it is completed. He sees how beautiful the tapestry is becoming right now, but we only see the loose ends and unfinished, messy back portion. Our role is to ask, to seek, to knock, and then to trust His plan. *"Trust in the LORD with all your heart and lean not on your own understanding"* (Prov. 3:5) Trust that the tapestry He is weaving in your life will indeed be beautiful! There may be a greater goal and plan that He has for you that you simply cannot see at this time!

What do we do when the miracle does not happen? When the healing doesn't come? Or when it doesn't come quickly enough? We pray for something we believe is in God's will, and still there is a long and difficult waiting period. When everything is stripped away, when our dreams are completely shattered, when the pain is so deep we can barely breathe, when we have emotionally hit rock bottom, if we reach out in our pain, we will discover that God is *there*! And we have the amazing opportunity to truly *lean on Him* because there is nothing else! We truly discovery that He will never leave us. We come to know Him in a deep, heartfelt way that could not have been possible if we had not experienced the pain that got us there.

God's word tells us to continue to pray "without ceasing." We hang on to our knowledge that God has a plan, to trust in that plan, *to lean on that plan,* and to know that He will answer in His way and in His timing. *"Be joyful in hope, patient in affliction, faithful in prayer"* (Rom. 12:12).

This is my story of sudden *life-threatening catastrophic illness, paralysis,* and *recovery.* I suffered a deadly illness, coma, and terrifying paralysis that lasted for a year. I had to wait for God's timing, and He rewarded me with full recovery and a deep relationship with Him. He promises you the same relationship to you! My prayer is that my story will encourage you as you trust and hope in our Lord and Savior to grant your miracle and meet your needs.

Let's take a look at how God creates a miracle for a man in the Bible who waited over forty years:

> *One day Peter and John were going up to the temple at the time of prayer—at three in the afternoon. Now a man who was lame from birth was being carried to the temple gate called Beautiful, where he was put every day to beg from those going into the temple courts. When he saw Peter and John about to enter, he asked them for money. Peter looked straight at him, as did John. Then Peter said, "Look at us!" So the man gave them his attention, expecting to get something from them. Then Peter said, "Silver or gold I do not have, but what I do have I give you. In the name of Jesus Christ of Nazareth, walk." Taking him by the right hand, he helped him up, and instantly the man's feet and ankles became strong. He jumped to his feet and began to walk. Then he went with them into the temple courts, walking and jumping, and praising God. When all the people saw him walking and praising God, they recognized him as the same man who used to sit begging at the temple gate called Beautiful, and they were filled with wonder and amazement at what had happened to him.*
>
> *When Peter saw this, he said to them: "Fellow Israelites, why does this surprise you? Why do you stare at us as if by our own power or godliness we had made this man walk? The God of Abraham, Isaac and Jacob, the God of our fathers, has glorified his servant Jesus.*

We are witnesses of this. By faith in the name of Jesus, this man whom you see and know was made strong. It is Jesus' name and the faith that comes through him that has completely healed him, as you can all see. (Acts 3:1–16)

In this story, *the lame man was healed in God's timing and to His glory*, so all people could see that He was the Almighty God. Hebrew 11 tells us, *"We walk by faith, not by sight."* My journey to recovery took faith! Writing a book takes faith! I invite you to come along with me on this journey as we explore God's promises of hope as He leads us toward healing! We walk by faith, not by sight.

Introduction

A Posting on Facebook

When the following brief paragraph was posted on a closed group on Facebook limited to vasculitis patients and families, summarizing the story of my sudden illness and remarkable recovery, I received over one hundred likes and fifty comments saying things like "You are such a fighter," "Congrats on fighting through it," "Stay strong," "and "Your story gives me hope."

> *Hi, I was perfectly fine, never sick, working full time in a corporate office for 26 years. One day in July 2014, I got a cold which rapidly became a deep cough, deep voice, and extreme fatigue and weakness. On the third day, I collapsed and was rushed to the ER unable to breathe. No memories after that but I was put on a respirator, got a tracheostomy, a feeding tube, a permanent IV line, and spent a month in ICU in a medically-induced coma as they tried to save my life. I developed ARDS and my white blood cell count went through the roof, but they didn't know why. The pulmonologist had to manually clean and clear my lungs several times. He told my husband that if my*

lungs closed, they would lose me. I was given nitric oxide because my lungs were not accepting oxygen. All organs were affected. For three days in ICU I was receiving 1,000 mg of prednisone a day, as well as many other drugs. My body puffed up from massive amounts of steroids and my lung popped. I had three rounds of dialysis, six pints of blood, kidney failure, a-fib in my heart, plasmapheresis, bronchoscopy, all while my family stood by, praying and watching helplessly. I went from never sick a day to on my death bed in a few days. Finally a kidney biopsy was sent to Mayo clinic and the diagnosis was made of Microscopic Polyangitis, or MPA, a form of vasculitis. They started an accepted protocol of Cytoxan, high dosage of prednisone, and other drugs and finally my numbers started to slowly improve. The diagnosis was made after 10 days in a coma in ICU. Then another 20 days in ICU for intensive treatment and stabilization, all in a coma. When I woke up on the 30th day, I could not breathe on my own, could not speak, could not eat or drink, and could not move a muscle, not even to turn my head. My mouth and lips were bone dry, but I was not allowed to have anything to drink. I had complete myopathy. I spent the next three months in a nursing home, and then was moved to my home, still unable to move or even to eat by myself. My family cared for my every need, and I received home nursing care, and physical and occupational therapy for the next 10 months. Recovery was very slow. Finally after one full year, I was able to walk up the stairs to

my own bedroom which I had not seen for a year!
I was able to take a shower in my own bathroom
at last. I am now recovered and healed praise God,
through God's grace and mercy, and the power of
prayer. It has been the hardest year of my life. A
long journey!!!

That the story of my illness generated so many responses was a surprise, as this was posted on a closed group and was not visible to anyone other than the members of this group. Yet this volume of response indicates that many people are struggling with serious health issues as well as other difficulties, and find strength and encouragement from the stories of others who have been in that battlefield, fought the good fight, trusted God, and have been healed. People are suffering and crying out for something to believe in, some port in the storms of life, something to hang onto. God is that *strong tower!* He will be our strength, He will carry us through, and He will show us the way to stay strong. It is my prayer that my story will provide reality, hope, encouragement, and a tribute to the power of prayer. God's promises are true and they come to life when we ask and trust Him! This is a story of suffering and heartbreak, but also of God's grace, mercy, strength, and sufficiency.

The Bible has many recorded incidents of God revealing His glory and power through healing. Acts 3 tells the story of a paralyzed man who was healed by Apostles Peter and John in the early days of the church. Because the crippled man had been paralyzed his whole life, the people in the area knew him as he begged daily at the temple gate. No doubt he questioned his circumstances as he prayed and hoped for healing at many times, only to find himself still crippled and begging at the temple gate. The crippled beggar could not see what God had in store for him. We don't see the whole picture the way God does. When we are asking for something, we only see part of the plan. The Bible says it is as if we "see through the glass darkly." The lame beggar in Acts 3 never knew what God had in store that day! God had a plan for his life as He does for every one of us, and when the time came, he was *healed!* This crippled man became a witness through his healing to the glory and incredible power of God.

Because our God is all-powerful, He can heal in many ways. My illness was very sudden and life-threatening and greatly impacted my family, friends, and work colleagues. Throughout the first month, I was near death, and my survival was in doubt. Multitudes of friends, family members, acquaintances, and church members throughout the country were praying for me. Administrators and others from my place of employment gathered in the chapel at the hospital, wept openly and prayed for my survival. A church pastor was interceding for me daily. He prayed that the Lord might allow my spirit to reenter my body. This pastor prayed by phone with my family in my hospital room. My family constantly played some of my favorite Christian praise music.

In time, and with an eventual proper diagnosis, medications helped me to become stable, and I was able to survive the most acute, life-threatening part of my illness. However, God had more in store for me. My healing did not come right away and took over a year of intensive rehabilitation. Although my healing did not come in an instant, it is miraculous in a different way. Today I am recovered and healed, and telling my story so others will see the glory of God! God had a plan for my life that would take me through a long journey of hope, trust, strength, and intimacy with our Lord and Savior.

My story is a modern-day miracle, a version of Acts 3 sprung to life in our modern, sophisticated, high-tech world. My miracle took place within a process of learning and trusting God, and this is the story of my journey. Just as my illness impacted many, my healing journey and my recovery miracle has touched many lives and testified to the glory and power of God. My whole story points directly to God! Best of all, it is a story of God's love and healing power that is available to all who ask and believe!

CHAPTER 1

My Grace Is Sufficient for You

My grace is sufficient for you, for my power
is made perfect in your weakness.
—2 Corinthians 12:9

Sometimes we can clearly feel the hand of God working in our lives. People sometimes refer to these circumstances or events as "God things." In reality, all of life is a God thing. He tells us that He has plans for us, and if we truly look with open eyes, sometimes we can clearly see that He is working for us.

Have you ever felt led to follow a certain path, to take a certain job, to be part of a certain organization? As if God is telling you, "You belong there!" Or have you worked in a position that felt like your niche, what you were put on earth to do? Well, I had the pleasure of having that position for twenty-six years as an employee of a large local Christian-based child care chain serving over 1,500 children and employing over 200 staff members at the time of my employment. The last several years I served as chief operating officer. What could ever be better than teaching children, working with people, helping families, and glorifying God? I loved it!

My tenure with the company began when my daughter attended preschool in the late '80s. My husband was transferred to Toledo, Ohio, from our hometown of Cleveland, and we moved to new city with our two little girls ages two and four. We knew no one and had no family near but quickly became friends with neighbors who also had two little girls. Their children attended a child care center, and they recommended that I consider it as a preschool for my younger daughter. One look and I knew we belonged there! I enrolled my daughter, and began working part time at the center.

I soon became prekindergarten teacher and then advanced to the positions of kindergarten teacher, administrator, human resource manager, vice president, and finally chief operating officer. My office was located in our corporate site but also involved some travel to our local sites as well as sites out of state. Each position offered new challenges, new opportunities, and new ways to reach people for Christ. One goal of the company was that each child would hear the name of Jesus from infancy through age ten. At the time of my illness, the company was in its thirty-second year of operation. I had been there since the company was about six years old, so I had the opportunity and privilege to help in building much of the infrastructure, systems, and substance.

In the role of COO, I was able to visit centers, observe classrooms, work with teachers, and enjoy the children as they learned and developed in a high-quality, beautiful, creative, and Christian environment. Our teaching philosophy was inspired by the Reggio approach (see appendix C) and centered on building relationships, respecting children, and recognizing children's inherent value and ability. Our classroom environments were structured in such a way as to encourage social learning among the children and stimulate creativity. Realizing that creativity, collaboration, and exploration are inherent in a high quality early learning program, our classrooms were also designed to be aesthetically beautiful and unique. Children and parents alike felt welcome and nurtured in this special space.

Part of my role as supervisor was to ensure that our educational content was meeting established benchmarks, programming was happening according to company standards, and teacher-child relationships were loving and strong. I ensured that every Friday morning, each classroom taught a "chapel lesson" focusing on how God loves us, makes each of us special, and is the Creator of the world. Children prayed before snacks and meals. Families were given great importance, and good customer service was required. Giving high priority to following state regulations and company standards, my role was to circulate among the centers offering support as well as maintaining the highest standards. This created a loving, nurturing, home-like atmosphere for the children. What a blessing!

As a corporate manager I was also expected to deal with difficult situations. Many times if parents were not satisfied or if teachers were not performing adequately or if children were injured, the situation would call for my intervention. In those situations, it was imperative to act as Christ would have acted, showing mercy and compassion to all. I believe firmly that our actions speak louder than our words.

My job included interviewing potential candidates for employment, conducting orientations, offering trainings for new teachers, supervising center directors, taking part in leadership team meetings, and representing our company in various groups and boards throughout the state. Many staff members would tell me later that they remembered how comfortable and welcome they felt in their interview with me. They saw our commitment to lifting staff members and families up in prayer, as well as bonding together as part of a united body of employees.

Although my position required some local as well as distant travel, some of my most significant travel experiences were to Romania. In an effort to give back to God, the owner of the company pursued a mission outreach to the orphans and underprivileged people in Romania. Through past relationships, she was connected to a college in Boston that had established a social-work training program in Romania as part of a "semester abroad" learning experience for students. A professor in Romania taught the students regular coursework while they engaged in hands-on learning experiences in the orphanages and with needy citizens of the town. A charity organization was established by the owner of our company, which drew many churches and mission teams to support the ministry. Our company, as well as the owner herself, began supporting her Romanian outreach with dollars, prayers, and team visits.

I was able to visit Romania twice, and it changed my life forever. The poverty of the gypsies, the plight of the orphans, and struggles of some of the townspeople was heartbreaking. As an early childhood educator, I was deeply affected by living conditions of babies and children in the orphanages, who suffered permanent damage from deplorable surroundings and lack of emotional support. Clearly God was calling us to expand our efforts to heal His children. The owner continues her work in Romania to this day and has supported and nourished the citizens in miraculous ways.

In 2008, several of us from the company collaborated to create a book highlighting the creative and unique early childhood environments within our schools. Together, the five of us captured the essence of how to design and enliven a responsive, stimulating environment for young children. Entitled *Inspiring Spaces for Young Children*, the book was published in 2010 and enjoyed wide acclaim as an inspiration for many teachers and directors to take their classroom environments to a higher level. After the publication, we offered many workshops and training based upon the design principles contained in the book. Thus, we were able to share our love for high quality early childhood environments with others in our field. This was another great blessing for our company.

In 2013, the outreach of our child care program was expanded out of state. The company opened a center in South Carolina, which was a challenge in terms of work, licensing rules and staffing issues. God was part of the design from the very beginning, and this center is not only flourishing but has been joined by another new center in the area because of the overwhelming demand. The centers are beautiful, loving, well-staffed, high quality educationally, and honor the name of Jesus. What a blessing and honor to God!

Throughout my twenty-six years with the company, the Lord was teaching me and calling me closer to Him. Our meetings always began with prayer, and Christian resources were shared by management, including a weekly prayer journal, which I circulated among our centers. I often prayed for employees or parents who were struggling in some way. I recognized and valued the platform that I had as a corporate manager, reflecting God in my daily activities and outreach. Our motto was to honor God in all we do. I rarely took a sick day. I loved my job, and I was blessed to be in good health, making efforts to exercise and eat properly. All of that was about to change. We never know what the future holds. The urgency of time was a lesson that I was to learn in a very personal way.

The second week of July 2014 was beginning with fairly typical weather and promised to be warm with lots of sunshine. Monday morning dawned as a bright, breezy July day. The administrator of our newest center out of state was visiting the previous week. We had just celebrated Independence Day the previous weekend at the lake-house retreat of the company president, enjoying boat rides and grilled hamburgers.

As the week began, I noticed that I had a strange cough and was feeling very tired. Of course, I continued to go to my office daily, thinking I would be fine. My coworkers kept giving me cough drops, and by Wednesday, I was at the doctor's office, where they did X-rays and diagnosed pneumonia. I was so weak I could barely walk out of the office without holding onto walls. In retrospect, I should have been sent straight to the ER!

I diligently took antibiotics and slept round the clock, but by Thursday, my condition had worsened. I was indescribably weak! It was an effort to hold my head up, and I wanted to just sink into my bed. I rode in the passenger side of my car on an important errand with my daughter, and when I tried to step out of the car, I collapsed on the garage floor like a rag doll. I simply had no energy, no awareness of my body in space, and my legs were like Jell-O. I remember thinking, *It's so nice and cool I'll just sleep here*—on the garage floor! Fortunately, my daughter was able to run around to my side of the car and actually catch my head before I fell to the ground. I have been blessed by my family in so many ways!

My daughter Allison and my husband, Ryan, helped me into the house, thinking I was just tired. Since I was still conscious, my husband drove me to the ER himself rather than calling 911. We never imagined how seriously ill I was. I prayed they would give me stronger medicine in ER and send me home so I could feel better and get back to work next week! I had things to do! Ryan brought me to the check-in desk of the ER in a wheelchair, and the nurse remarked "You don't look sick." I'll never forget thinking, *She must think I am faking this?* Looks can be deceiving! By this time, I could not breathe, and my blood oxygen level had dropped to the 80s. This had to be more than pneumonia. My lungs were closing. I could barely sit up straight.

When I was taken back to an examining room, the nurse tried to put an oxygen mask over my face and I fought vehemently. I thought she was suffocating me! I knew I could not breathe, and my thinking was becoming fuzzy. Who were all these people? Where was I? I was beginning to lose consciousness, yet the nurses were asking me questions. What medications did I take? What have I taken recently? Fortunately, I carried a medication card in my wallet and was able to direct the nurse to that. At this point, I was drifting in and out of consciousness. I would put my head back down on the examining table and pass out.

The Lord tells us in His Word that "my grace is sufficient for you, for my power is made perfect in your weakness" (2 Cor. 12:9). I was at the weakest point physically I had ever been in my life. What was going on? I was totally dependent on God!!

CHAPTER 2

A Month-Long Coma

The Lord will protect him and preserve his life... the Lord will
sustain him on his sickbed and restore him from his bed of illness.
—Psalm 41:2–3

When I collapsed at home, fortunately my husband and daughter were beside me. If I had been home alone, I might have died right there in my garage because my blood-oxygen level was so low I was losing consciousness. Because of my family, I was in the hospital emergency room. I was unable to breathe well or to stay awake. Although I was not in pain, I was not fully conscious. I could hear my husband speaking with the doctors, and I had an overwhelming urge to just run away! This was the last place that I wanted to be. I was becoming completely helpless as doctors spoke with my family about the best treatment options. I was moved from ER to the intensive care unit (ICU) on the second floor of the hospital soon after my admission. My condition was very serious, and I was being watched closely for any signs of improvement. The doctors fully expected the drugs they administered to be effective. I would later tell my husband that I had no memory of anything after the ER.

By this time, my husband had contacted my daughter Jennifer, who is married and lives in Tennessee. Since the doctors were still assuming this was pneumonia, Ryan was unable to tell Jen much about my prognosis. "Dad, do you think I should come up there?" she asked. Jen is married and was a student at University of Tennessee studying nutrition, and her schedule was hectic. The drive from Knoxville to Toledo was seven hours one way. Since I had no previous chronic medical conditions and had never been hospitalized other than the birth of my children, Ryan suggested they wait and see what the day and night would bring.

The medical team was evaluating my condition and administering standard protocol for treating pneumonia, including giving massive antibiotics and fluids, monitoring the blood-oxygen level, and looking for improvement. In general, pneumonia will respond to this treatment. However, over the next twenty-four to thirty-six hours, my condition worsened substantially. An infectious disease specialist was called in to consult, thinking that perhaps this was pneumonia caused by a different strain of bacteria. Some types of bacteria are especially resistant to treatment, and this option was explored. No other type of bacteria was identified.

The doctors told my husband they might have to intubate because my lungs were not accepting oxygen. One doctor said, "If her lungs close, we will lose her." My husband remembered that his knees became weak as he realized the doctor was saying I was close to death! I was very weak, and God would have to be my strength! My husband gave permission for the doctors to induce a medical coma, which would keep me still and out of pain. The medical team administered Nimbex and Propofol, a general anesthetic often used for critically ill patients who require a breathing tube connected to a ventilator. Michael Jackson died from an overdose of Propofol in 2009. Although this was the only option at the time, it was a decision that would have great ramifications later.

In addition to trying to process and understand what was happening to me, my husband took on the roles of advocate and communication director. He talked to Jennifer in Tennessee and told her what was happening, and she decided to leave for Toledo immediately. A seven-hour drive took her only five hours, amid tears and phone calls to Ryan and to her husband, Alan. Her greatest fear is that I would not survive until she arrived.

Ryan also began notifying my employer, family, and friends of the seriousness of the situation. In one of the early messages, my employer asked if I would be well enough to return to work within two weeks or so. Ryan had no answer at the time. Later we would remark about how unexpected and unprepared we were for a situation this unusual and devastating.

People who learned of my condition began showering us with meals, cards, visits, and prayers. Everyone was in shock! My dear friends at work started bringing meals to my family at the hospital every day. I would later learn from my family how much they enjoyed the tasty Italian foods, stuffed breadsticks, pizza, as well as many homemade dishes that were supplied. The administrators of the childcare company where I was employed took shifts, rotating the responsibility of providing meals, as their way of supporting me and my family. They also visited the chapel of the hospital and prayed for me. I was told that there were many tears shed. A pastor named Carlos, who was a friend of my employer, began praying for me. Because he was out of state, he was leading prayer as the administrators were in the chapel praying. Carlos prayed to God that "my spirit would return to my body."

The prayers that were offered and the love and caring actions of my friends and coworkers supported my family as they endured a daily struggle with hearing "no improvement" and even worse news. Later I would tell everyone that these prayers were God's love washing over me and healing me. He works through the people in our lives, and He answers prayer. I know now that although we do not see and cannot touch God, we experience his love and his healing power through the prayers of those who love us. Truly they are God's hands extended here on earth.

My condition was deteriorating. Although the hospital had assembled a team of medical doctors covering every discipline—pulmonologist, nephrologist, hematologist, neurologist, rheumatologist, cardiologist, infectious-disease specialist—and more, the cause of my condition could not be identified. Within twenty-four hours, I was put on a ventilator for life support. Initially they started with a lower amount of oxygen, but it was too slow. They had to adjust the ventilator to keep the alveoli in my lungs open and manipulate the oxygen, which was up to 100 percent at certain points.

It was rapidly determined that I had developed ARDS, acute respiratory distress syndrome (see appendix A). This is an extremely serious, often fatal, condition. The doctor later told my husband that ARDS is thought to have up to a 90 percent mortality rate. ARDS typically occurs in people who are already critically ill or who have significant injuries. It happens when fluid builds up in the tiny, elastic air sacs (alveoli) in the lungs. This fluid builds up when small blood vessels leak fluid into the tiny air sacs. Severe injury or inflammation undermines the integrity of the membranes keeping the fluid in place. More fluid in the lungs means less oxygen can reach the bloodstream. This deprives the organs of the oxygen they need to function. Severe shortness of breath—the main symptom of ARDS—usually develops within a few hours after the original disease or trauma.

Many people who develop ARDS do not survive, and those who do often experience lasting damage to their lungs. The risk of death increases with age and severity of illness. I would later hear my doctor saying, "You have a better prognosis because you are young and healthy." At the time, I did not feel young and I certainly did not feel healthy!

31

At this point, I had been in the ICU for over twenty-four hours, and doctors were attempting to diagnose what was happening. They had diagnosed ARDS but still thought it was due to pneumonia. They continued to administer megadoses of antibiotics, while they tried to reduce the fluid buildup in my lungs. Cultures were taken from my lungs to determine what kind of bacteria was present so it could be treated properly. Clearly, the antibiotics were not working as they should have been, and my condition continued to deteriorate.

Because of continued intense inflammation of lung tissue, the doctors administered large doses of 1,000 mg of the steroid Prednisone for three days. This in turn led to swelling which made my lung "pop," sending air into my upper torso as determined by a CT scan. My whole body blew up like a balloon! My husband and children were weak with concern and exhaustion. They tried to support each other through this awful time by telling stories and recalling things from the past.

The pulmonologist performed a "bronchoscopy," in which he suctioned out material from the lungs in an effort to allow oxygen to enter. This is a procedure in which a hollow, flexible tube called a bronchoscope is inserted into the airways through the nose or mouth to provide a view of the tracheobronchial tree. It is also used to collect bronchial and/or lung secretions and to perform tissue biopsy. My lungs were as hard as rocks, which can be deadly. Because my lungs were so deeply affected, a biopsy would later be done using tissue from my kidneys, so as not to damage the lungs even further.

One treatment for ARDS is the use of nitric oxide, which is easier on the lungs and improves oxygenation. This is the type of oxygen often given to premature babies in the NICU (neonatal intensive care unit) and once I received nitric oxide, my lungs improved slightly. More oxygen was being transported into the bloodstream, and blood pressure readings became more stable. The key was for the lungs to get better and less rigid. This was very encouraging for the medical team as well as for my distraught family!

During my medically induced coma, the medical team was not able to move me in any way. My condition was so fragile and so severe that any movement, even turning me to the side, would cause the monitor reading to fluctuate wildly. My blood pressure would go through the roof. Because of this, my body was left in a prone position, which led to a pressure sore on my lower back. This sore would cause much pain during my recovery process and would take months to heal, even causing me another trip to the ER!

By this time, we were five days into the medically induced coma. I was hooked up to multiple machines that were monitoring every bodily system (see picture). My family believed that I might be able to hear so they set up a CD player and continually played my favorite Christian praise music in my room. People from everywhere were praying and sending encouraging scripture verses to my husband. As our pastor friend prayed for me over the speaker phone, my family noted that my blood pressure readings improved! Even though I was not fully conscious, and my family was struggling with feelings of despair, somehow the Lord's presence was with us in that hospital room, and we were aware that Jesus was carrying us through this difficult time. God is so good!

One good friend texted the following: *"For surely O Lord you bless the righteous, you surround them with our favor as with a shield"* (Ps. 5:12). Another friend said she felt in her spirit that "all is well." These words, prayers, and thoughts were truly God's hands extended to my family as they stood watch beside me. One friend quipped, "When you are going through something hard and wonder where God is, remember the teacher is always quiet during a test!" Because of God's unfailing love, my husband was able to not only keep everyone updated with daily text blasts but to encourage them by saying, "If God is for us, who can be against?" Throughout the entire ordeal,

God held Ryan up by his victorious right hand so that he could be a rock for others. The strength and tenacity of my dear husband and children remains to me another miracle!

Day 6 of the coma brought the news that all the cultures that were taken did not grow anything! If it was not pneumonia, then what could be causing this dramatic, catastrophic illness in an otherwise healthy individual?? This was a puzzle for the medical personnel, some of whom had never seen anything of this kind. I was in a hospital that was not the largest hospital in my city, but a good hospital, nonetheless. I was blessed to have a skilled multidisciplinary team of physicians dedicated to discovering the root cause of my condition. Later I would learn that the medical notes of the thirty days I spent in the ICU would comprise 4,400 pages in my medical record! That is a lot of checking, examining, conferring, and writing!

Lasix, a diuretic, was utilized to reduce water saturation. As my oxygen levels continued to be low, more body systems were affected. Gradually, all body functions were affected. My kidneys began to fail. I would receive complete kidney dialysis six times during my time in the coma. The Lasix altered my electrolytes so they had to back off them. The pulmonologist, renal doctor, hematologist, and rheumatologist together found a correlation where antibodies were attacking the microscopic and small blood vessels in the lungs and kidneys. This was the first indication of a future diagnosis that would save my life. But there was still much work to be done, beginning with plasmapheresis.

Plasmapheresis is a method of removing blood plasma from the body by withdrawing blood, separating it into plasma and cells, and transfusing the cells back into the bloodstream. This is performed to remove antibodies that are attacking the body, and is used primarily in autoimmune conditions. It is administered by the Red Cross, taking several hours, by inserting a catheter into the bloodstream and replacing the plasma. The medical team began to assert that antibodies were the culprit attacking the blood vessels in my lungs and kidneys, but to confirm the diagnosis, they needed to do a biopsy. Because my lungs were so affected and a biopsy would be risky, they took several biopsies of my kidneys and sent them to Mayo Clinic for final diagnosis.

By the end of this ordeal, I would have four rounds of plasma-pheresis to clean the blood of antibodies. In addition, the medical team started dialysis to remove any toxins built up in the kidneys. To this day, I marvel at the miraculous ways our Creator has designed for our bodies to function and the role that each organ has in clean-ing, nourishing, and sustaining life. Rather than a random act of intelligent design, it is clear that "we are fearfully and wonderfully made" by our Heavenly Father who loves us so much. I praise God daily that He gave my medical team the skill, knowledge, and perse-verance to solve the puzzle of my illness!

By the eighth day of my coma, there were small signs of some improvement. Oxygen tank was reduced to 55 percent, nitric oxide was required now at 2.5 ppm (down from 20 ppm) and swelling was reduced. I had received a feeding tube in my stomach, which allowed continuous nutrition and medication. X-rays continued to be slightly better, and my family and friends were encouraged. Still no official diagnosis, but doctors felt strongly that immune-suppres-sants would help. A main goal was to wean me from the nitric oxide and go to regular oxygen. They were taking baby steps.

Day 10 of the coma brought a new complication! Because of all that my body had been through, I developed atrial fibrillation, which is an irregular, often rapid heart rate that commonly causes poor blood flow. This is a potentially life-threatening condition that can lead to stroke. The various treatments used in my illness were thought to be taxing on my body, and the cardiologist administered medication and suggested a day of rest from treatments.

Throughout the time I spent in ICU in a coma, my husband continued his text blasts to a large network of friends and family, who all in turn kept a constant prayer vigil on our behalf. He was like a rock for all those around him who marveled at his faith and strength. I know in my heart that it is the continuous, fervent prayers of dear friends that washed over us and healed me! Those who prayed for me were also praying for strength for my family and especially my husband. God answered those prayers a hundred fold. God says, "The fervent prayer of a righteous man avails much." I know this is why I am healed today!

The next four long days would see more dialysis, plasmapheresis, and suctioning of my lungs as they waited patiently for the formal diagnosis from the Mayo Clinic. I continued in critical condition on a roller coaster of low hemoglobin counts, periodic atrial fibrillation, and bleeding. All told, I received six units of blood and became allergic to heparin, a blood thinner. Since my platelets dropped, they switched to argatroban, a different type of blood thinner. They also began treatment with an immune-suppressant drug called Cytoxan, which is actually a chemotherapy drug. Because I was so very sick, I could not have visitors other than family, and when anyone came into the room, they had to wear a gown and mask. My immune system was being suppressed, and I could not tolerate any types of germs. This infectious-disease precaution continued for several months.

Now it had been many days that I was in ICU, and my family was becoming exhausted. They took turns going home to take a shower, change clothes, and get some sleep. My husband slept primarily in recliner near my room. Because of the generosity of friends, there was always plenty of food available. My son's coworkers cooked and baked meals for him to share with us. My daughter Jen loves to bake, and when she took some time at home, she baked to relieve her stress and fear. She proudly brought muffins and other treats to share with others. My family shared some with the nursing staff who attended me so closely. In my time in the ICU, I would have over twenty nurses and assistants on my case. My husband had already taken two unpaid weeks off work and completed FMLA paperwork allowing him more time. He showered and dressed, came to the hospital, went to work for eight hours, then came back to the hospital. This continued for weeks. The prayers of those who cared for me and God's grace kept him strong!

Finally, on July 24, 2014, fourteen days after being admitted to ICU and put on life support and still in a coma, we received the official diagnosis of *vasculitis* (see appendix B). This is an autoimmune disorder that attacked my lungs and caused my kidneys to fail. Vasculitis is a category of autoimmune disorders defined as an inflammation of the blood vessels that causes changes in the blood vessel walls, decreasing blood flow. It is rare with fewer than two hundred thousand cases each year in the United States. It cannot be cured, but treatment can help. In addition, my particular form of vasculitis is MPA, or microscopic polyangitis, a "small vessel" vasculitis affecting the arterioles (small arteries), capillaries, and venules (small veins). The areas most often affected are kidneys, lungs, nerves, skin, and joints. No wonder the doctors were baffled!

Once the diagnosis was confirmed, a standard course of treatment could be followed. The normal protocol in this case was Prednisone and Cytoxan. These treatments proved to be effective in the long run at lowering inflammation and reducing white blood cell count, which had been through the roof. But we were not yet out of the woods!

Beginning on day 16, with course of treatment begun, the doctors started discussing lowering the sedatives used to keep me in a coma. This process alone would take about ten days, as I was in stable but critical condition. Dialysis continued as well as plasmapheresis, but at least it seemed there was an end in sight. ARDS was still impacting my condition but getting better by the day. On day 18, the doctor declared, "Mary Ann is not in ARDS now!" This brought huge relief to my family, friends, and medical team. With prayers of many people and tremendous faith of my family and friends, God had brought me through one storm and the doctors could breathe a sigh of relief. My pulmonologist said, "It is a miracle!"

On day 19, the medical team began to wean me very slowly from the sedatives. They had slowly reduced the paralytic Nimbex, which allowed me to very gradually wake up over the course of several days. Doctors continued to monitor my heart rate, blood pressure, kidney function, and lung capacity. Oxygen had been decreased, as well as the need for plasmapheresis and dialysis. By July 29, the twentieth day, there had been significant vasculitis improvement in lungs and kidneys and reduction of inflammation.

Finally on July 30, with sedation at its minimum level, I began to slowly open my eyes. I was very groggy and in a dreamlike state. Weaning down was still a slow process, as they tried to get me off the ventilator and breathing on my own. This was very touch-and-go and monitored closely. The vent was still giving me six breaths per minute, but I could also breathe on my own. They were waiting for me to be able to breathe entirely on my own to eliminate the vent entirely. My husband told me that it was like a new baby being born—everyone waits for the "cry" to make sure the baby can breathe! Well, sorry to disappoint, but I didn't have the strength to cry!

Although I was gradually awakening, and my body was responding to treatment, in many ways, this was just the beginning of the miracle. You see, when I awoke from the medically induced coma, I was unable to move at all. I was not even able to turn my head. I had profound myopathy. The combination of a month of paralytic medication, no movement, and ARDS rendered me virtually paralyzed. When I was fully awake, I could not breathe yet on my own, could not speak, eat, drink, or move at all. My family attempted to communicate with me through eye blinks—one for yes, two for no.

That was the only way I could let them know I recognized them. So even though I had survived the critical acute state of ICU and being in a coma, my ordeal was far from over. In some ways, it was just beginning. The next year would be round two of my miracle. I was totally dependent on God!!

By August 1, the doctors felt my breathing trials were going well, white blood cell counts were better, and I was on the mend. Again, the doctors told my husband, "This is truly a miracle!" Although I could see a little and recognized my family, I was still in a dreamlike state. My first conscious memory upon awakening was hearing on the TV that Toledo was in a water crisis! People in Toledo were told, "Don't drink the water!" I was still only semiconscious, and I thought, *Oh my gosh, it must be the end of the world!* But I had no way to communicate those fears. My family tried to communicate with me using a sheet of paper with the alphabet—I would try to say something, and my husband would try to spell it out using the letters. Because I was so weak, this was too overwhelming, and we gave it up.

I also had vague memories of a nightmare I had while I was still in a coma. I saw myself in a hospital, but I didn't want to be there. I kept saying, "Let me out of here!" My husband was standing beside me like a sentinel, looking straight ahead and not saying a word. I kept telling him, "C'mon! C'mon, Pookey! Let's get out of here. We can go out those side windows. No one will notice! Let's go!" I was shouting in my dream, but he didn't even look at me! Very frustrating and disturbing feelings surrounded me when I woke up. We later thought that because I was fighting the attempts at the oxygen mask when I was admitted, and I was so weak and fearful, perhaps this fear carried over into my dream. Perhaps it was a premonition of sorts, because when I awoke, I would not be able to walk for a year!

I was satisfied only when my family was by my side at every moment, as I felt very frightened and alone. While relief and joy were palpable in the medical team and in my family, we all knew this was just the beginning. Somewhat like surviving a hurricane, relief comes when you have survived the storm, but the cleanup still follows. The doctors emphasized that I had a long way to go, but they felt that full recovery was possible. Plans were being made for me to transfer to a rehab facility within a few days for continued monitoring, physical and occupational therapy. The road ahead would be very long. A new phase of my life had begun!

CHAPTER 3

In the Center
of His Will

*When you search for me, you will find me, if
you seek me with all your heart.*
—Jeremiah 29:13

Some people have interesting, dynamic stories to tell about when they first met Jesus. Sometimes it was the result of a testimony they heard at a religious service, a very charismatic speaker, a significant person in their life, or a conversion experience after facing hardship or trouble. God wants to draw each of us close to Him and will do so in any way possible. My parents were religious people, and I was raised in the Catholic faith. I knew about Jesus from a very early age and attended Catholic schools for sixteen years. In addition to a solid education, I received instruction in the Bible and in the tenets of Catholicism. My mother was a sweet, loving woman whose life centered around her family and church. Since my mom did not drive, we walked everywhere, and every time we passed a church, we would go inside for a short prayer. Also, if an ambulance went screaming past us, we would automatically pray for the person inside and his family. I still do that to this day! Early habits last a lifetime.

My mother always looked to Jesus in her everyday life. If something was lost in the house, she asked Jesus to help her find it! Her favorite verse was *"See! I have engraved you on the palms of my hands, your walls are ever before me"* (Isa. 49:16). A special time for me was when I received the sacraments as part of my religious schooling. My First Communion day was simply magical. I see these experiences now as a foreshadowing of what was to come in my life, a foundation of faith for what God had planned for my future.

But knowing *about* Jesus and *knowing Jesus are two different things.* I am grateful for my childhood experiences, but I am even more grateful for how I would experience the depth and breadth of His love as an adult. In my early twenties as a newly married woman, I made a retreat at which I came face-to-face with the experience of knowing Jesus. We spoke about Jesus as a personal Savior, related stories of how He was working in our lives, and discussed passages from a new perspective. Jesus touched my heart in a new way that weekend, and I felt like I was soaring. As I read the scripture, *"If you declare with your mouth 'Jesus is Lord', and believe in your heart that God raised him from the dead, you will be saved"* (Rom. 10:9), suddenly Jesus became *alive* to me! My eyes were opened, and I saw completely and beautifully that He is my personal savior, that He died for *me*, and I am saved! If I were the only person on earth, He would have done the same to save just me! Experiencing this truth in my heart opened a new chapter in my life that would never be the same.

From that point on, I read the scriptures voraciously, seeking to know my Jesus better and better as He revealed Himself through His precious word. *I prayed to be in the center of His will* and always to make my life pleasing to Him. Throughout my life I came to know Jesus more and more as a personal savior, and even in the darkest days following my illness, He reassured me that "I have brought you this far, I will not abandon you now."

Through all the experiences of my life, I felt God drawing me closer and closer to Him. So although Jesus was a strong force carrying me through all the circumstances of my life, and His love grew stronger with each passing year, nothing had prepared me for the type of dependence and surrender that I would experience through this illness and gradual recovery period. Because I knew Jesus, He continued to carry me and provide that safe harbor in the violent storm of an illness that would almost consume me.

It was my faith in God's goodness and power that saved me from utter hopelessness in the days following my coma in which I could not move or speak. When I first woke from the medically-induced coma, and was unable to move, speak or breathe, all I had was God! God was ever present in my heart and my mind, and I spoke to Him in my thoughts and spirit constantly. I was still in a mental fog. I asked why? Why did this happen to me? And the answer I received was 'why not you?' I immediately asked forgiveness for everything that I had done to fall short of the mercy of God. I asked God to help me and heal me, and from that moment, I was not alone. Although my recovery would prove to be slow, He was always with me. *"Faith is being sure of what we hope for, certain of what we do not see"* (Heb. 11:1).

As I gradually regained consciousness, I had two overwhelming thoughts. My first thought was, *This is God!* God is not tangible that we can touch Him; He is not clearly visible that we can see Him; for many, He is not even audible that we can hear Him as we do other people. *God is love!* He comes to us through the outpouring of love and thoughts and prayers of all of those who pray for us! God healed me through the prayers of the pastor who pleaded for my life, through my husband who kept the faith day by day and would not give up on me, through my amazing family who would not leave my side, through my dear friends who prayed without ceasing and did everything they could to show their love, through my extended

MARY ANN RODY

family across the country who prayed daily for my healing, through the doctors and nurses who used their God-given skills and deep concern to do the best for me and my family. *This is God!* God's love washed over me and healed me! This was God pouring himself into our world and showing us that He is *real!* No, not tangible, but real, nonetheless. I experienced his love and his healing in this way.

My second overwhelming thought was the *URGENCY OF TIME.* We have no guarantee that we will be alive tomorrow or even the next hour. Life is so fragile! I was relatively healthy, never taking sick time, feeling great, working full time, traveling. I tried to eat well and exercise. Yet I collapsed and was literally on my deathbed the next day. When we say good-bye to someone, we might never see them again. Of course, we know this is reality, but do we live in this knowledge? How many times do we part from our loved ones in anger? Yell at our children or husband before they leave the house? Argue with a friend on the phone and hang up on them? God is calling us to be more aware of our relationships and live and act in a way to honor them. What would you say to your husband or wife if you knew it would be the last time you saw them? To your children? To your friends, your employer?

The urgency of time had such a great impact on me that my husband and I called our attorney to come to my hospital room to make changes in our final papers that we had thought about but never did. While I was in the rehab hospital, our attorney came with new papers and my husband signed on my behalf with a power of attorney. We knew we had to get everything in order. Is your life in order? Trust me, you don't know what tomorrow will bring!

Later, Jesus would take me deeper into my spiritual journey as I prayed and meditated more. He assured me that this is a dark season, but there are so many treasures in this season just for me. He told me to have *faith* and *trust.* He was building these things in me as an example for many. I prayed, asking Jesus for less of me and more of

44

Him. Throughout my illness, my deep desire was that when people looked at me, they would see *Him.* Before I was able to speak, medical personnel would tell me I was doing so much better and that I was a strong person. Because I couldn't speak yet, I cried, and they didn't know why. It was because I wanted to shout, "No, I'm not strong! It is God doing the work in me!" Jesus was always with me and would be with me until the end of the age (Matt. 28:20).

The next days and months were excruciatingly difficult. I felt like a foreigner in a strange land! I would learn vocabulary and procedures that I had never heard of. Many trials remained, which would test my strength physically, mentally, and emotionally. I would later understand that Jesus had saved me during the most intense, near-death experience of my life, but He was not finished with me yet! At times, my relationship with Jesus was one of desperation—like I was drowning and He was extending the branch to pull me out of the water. I was hanging on for dear life! That is where Jesus met me—at the place where I was utterly alone.

Someone asked me recently if I ever lost my faith during this time. Absolutely not! My faith was *all* I had!!! He was literally my lifeline. I hung on like a drowning person, and Jesus never let me go! Hebrews 13 says, *"Never will I leave you or forsake you."* I clung to those words and learned that the promises of God are true! The next year would prove to be a profound test of my faith, perseverance, and trust in God.

CHAPTER 4

Life in a Nursing Home

O Lord, I call to you for help and you healed me.
—Psalm 30:2

When I learned I would be moved from the acute care hospital to the rehab, or step-down, hospital, I should have been thrilled, but I had mixed feelings. My pulmonologist was excited and said to me, "Mary Ann, today you and me, we are going to rehab!" Understandably, he was the primary doctor who saved my life by the grace of God. This was a day of victory for him, but I was still extremely groggy and somewhat fearful of what the future held. I felt as if I was in a dark forest with no flashlight. I would be moving forward with no idea of what lay ahead or even if I would be able to make it. All I knew was that I had no choice. I was fearful that the new facility would not be able to care for me—I was completely dependent! What if something happened to my heart? Or my lungs? Would I survive? Would they know what to do? Why couldn't I just stay in the hospital?

I have heard it said, "We are strong when strong is the only option!" From early on, many people encouraged me saying I was doing so well, I was such a fighter and that they admired my strength.

Ironically, this made me cry! I knew that I was not the strong one—it was God living in me! I wanted to shout that to everyone, but I could not speak. Again I had to lean on God to carry me forward to the next step of my recovery. God was teaching me to trust!

My daughters accompanied me when they transferred me to my first rehab hospital. The nurse showed us to my room and explained a bit about the procedures. It seemed much more relaxed than the acute care hospital, but I would still be hooked up to heart and breathing monitors. I was in a gurney as I could not sit upright and would not be able to for many months. The back of my bed was slightly elevated at a thirty-degree angle so I could see. Because I had total myopathy of my muscles, I could also not move or control any core muscles to keep me sitting up straight. At this point, I could not move my head, hands, legs, fingers—nothing. All of that was to come much, much later. I was still not permitted to have visitors as my condition was still critical, and I was being monitored daily. At the rehab hospital, I received a voice piece that someone could hold to my throat so I could make sounds with my mouth in a very low, raspy tone. Since I had been horizontal for a month by this time, I had also developed back sores, which had to be treated by a wound nurse.

My fondest memory at my first rehab hospital is being evaluated by the speech pathologist and learning that I could have ice chips. Since coming out of the coma several days earlier, I could not have anything by mouth because of the tracheostomy, so my mouth was extremely dry. Let's just say it was like a desert and all I could taste was sand! My lips were cracked and dry. I was being fed intravenously with a large "formula" bottle, and periodically the nurses would dip a small sponge into water to wet my lips. Also, part of the hygiene procedures was to wipe off my teeth with antiseptic mouthwash on a tiny sponge. That was a lot of fun! I didn't know at the time that it would be months before my teeth would ever be brushed. Therefore, ice chips sounded magical to me, and every person who came into my room was not permitted to leave until they gave me ice chips. I would not be able to feed myself for a very long time. Looking back, I see that God was teaching me about total surrender, dependence, and humility in a very real way!

As the days passed at rehab, my family was able to see slow progress. I had several sessions of physical therapy, sometimes twice a day, and electrical stimulation from a therapist in my own room. They were determined to wake those muscles up. When I say physical therapy, keep in mind that I could not move. Therapy consisted of putting electrodes on my inactive muscles and stimulating them with electricity. I could feel this, and I could tell the therapist when the current was too strong for me. These were positive signs. But the therapy was not physical by any stretch of the imagination! My muscles were completely dormant. One time, when an aide was putting socks on my feet in my room, she held my foot up for a moment to pull the sock on. As she did so, my calf skin hung limp and lifeless from my shin bone. I cried! My calf muscle seemed to no longer exist, replaced by flabby skin! What a visual reminder of how devastated my body had become by this illness.

Although I still had no movement, one day I was able to have my bed briefly propped up to a ninety-degree angle and could turn my head to the right. My therapist asked me to turn it to the left, and when I couldn't, he manually turned my head to the left! It did not hurt, but I thought my head would fall off! After that, I was able to turn my head in each direction. Baby steps and I had to be grateful for each one. But couldn't I progress a little faster?

Each day, I was taken to the physical therapy room, which consisted of a variety of machines. One day I saw several other patients receiving therapy, and because of my mental state, I became alarmed. It was the first time I came face-to-face with the realization of the extent of my condition. The other patients had very serious conditions, one being a young man with traumatic brain injury and one being a man who had lost his eye in an accident. The young man with TBI was being encouraged to remember his name. "You remember how to say it, right?" "You can say 'Tim.' Come on, try," or "Try to say 'Tim.'" And he looked on at them with no expression, unable to say his name. I remember thinking, *Why am I here? Am I this bad? Will I ever get better? What if I am like this forever?*

I began to have a panic attack and was taken back to my room. My nurse gave me a sedative. From then on, the physical and occupational therapist came to my room. I would have several more incidents of reality hitting me in the face during the long process of recovery. Gradually, I was coming to understand how gravely ill I was. It was a difficult road physically, mentally, and emotionally, but through all of it, Jesus was able to carry me through.

My medical situation was under intense scrutiny. Each day, my nurses checked monitors and recorded numbers, and several doctors checked with me daily. The speech pathologist spent a lot of time assessing my swallowing ability, because having a tracheostomy can damage your throat and cause you to aspirate food into your lungs. Therefore, I had several swallow tests, which involved inserting a tube, which had a fiber optic camera at the tip, into my throat through my nose. I was fed small portions of food, such as a tiny bite of cheese sandwich, small piece of cookie, etc., which I had to chew and swallow while the pathologist observed it passing down my throat all while the tube was in my nose. I had no idea such a form of torture was actually a medical procedure! Luckily, I calmed myself down enough to pass each of the swallow tests except the one with liquids. I was deemed able to eat solid foods, but I had to remain on thickened liquids until a later date. If you can imagine drinking coffee the consistency of mud, that was my fate! But it was progress!

Several visitors were allowed to see me as my condition was becoming more stable. Two dear friends of mine who worked with me came with smiles and small talk, which lifted my spirits. They also gave me a beautiful Celtic cross bracelet, and I can remember thinking, *Why are they giving me a bracelet? I'll never be able to wear it again.* Today, I wear that bracelet every day as a reminder of their sweet love and constant concern, which helped heal me. Another very dear friend from my office visited, and we spoke for a long time. After he left, he told me through an e-mail that I was "one amazing person" and he was glad to see me again. I reminded him that when he left my room, he was to wipe the hard drive in his brain of the memory of seeing me this way. He chuckled and said, "It's what's inside that counts, not what's on the outside." These simple words from dear friends bolstered my spirit and made me feel that I might survive this ordeal. The words we say to those in great misery hold the power of healing and encouragement. *"Therefore, encourage one another and build one another up, just as you are doing"* (1 Thess. 5:11).

Another time, I had a surprise visit from a woman representing a professional association to which I belonged. She stayed for a while and brought beautiful silk flowers. It lifted my spirits that people cared! Later after I recovered, she would tell me that she was quite shaken after the visit to see how much I had been impacted by the illness. The glory of God's healing power was shining through in my recovery.

At this time, I was still using oxygen but only at night through a tube in my nose. That would continue for many months as my lungs continued to heal from damage and scars. The doctors capped the tracheostomy in preparation for reversal a little ways down the road, and I continued to use the small mouthpiece to speak if someone else pressed it to my throat. I could speak very softly, but it was a relief to be able to communicate. I received another strong dose of Cytoxan, the chemotherapy drug that was being used to suppress my immune system, in addition to steroids. Later, I would learn that this drug would cause my hair to fall out and my bladder to bleed. Again, the pulmonologist told my husband, "Mary Ann's bounce back is a miracle!" I certainly did not feel that I was bouncing, but I was happy to hear his comment. Thank you, Jesus!

Toward the end of the month of August, the tracheostomy tube was removed completely, and the opening was predicted to heal within a week. Because the opening was so large, it took six weeks to heal completely. The nursed had to clean it with antiseptic each day and apply bandages, which hurt terribly when removed. They eventually left it open so it could heal in open air. When I tried to speak, this would cause a "flapping" of the skin around wound, which was very frustrating! Eventually, the opening healed, and I was able speak normally, but the whole process took two months. To this day, I have a tiny scar that I consider to be my badge of honor!

Since I was nonambulatory, I had a urine catheter, and it quickly became apparent that my bladder was bleeding. One of the attending physicians ordered that a scope of my bladder be performed in the hospital to determine if there was internal damage from the Cytoxan, as this is a known side effect. Another physician had ordered a drug called mesna to stop the bleeding in the short term, and I was transferred to the acute-care hospital on Sunday night to have the bladder scope on Monday morning.

When Monday morning came, the doctor said the bladder scope to determine the amount of damage to the bladder could no longer be performed. Apparently, the insurance company would not approve the bladder scope because the bleeding had stopped because of the Mesna! I was to be transferred back to the rehab hospital, and that would have been okay. But because the insurance company felt I was no longer in need of critical care, they would not allow me to be readmitted there! They could not take me back! If I was not a patient in need of critical care, I don't know who was! I was fighting an overwhelming autoimmune disease, recovering from ARDS, unable to move or speak! The nurses and caregivers had begun to develop relationships with me that I treasured, and I learned to trust them with my care. Now I was unable to go back or even to say good-bye. All my personal items had to be picked up by my family. I had nowhere to go!

Because of a glitch in communication and inherent bureaucracy in the health care system, I was left with nowhere to go for three days. One facility could not take me because I didn't need that much care, and another facility would not take me because I needed too much care! My mental state was very fragile, so I cried hard and often those three days, and the social worker on my case was very dedicated and sympathetic. I received pain killers to make me comfortable and sedatives to calm me down. My husband was with me the whole time as we searched frantically for a new location with the help of the social worker. Finally, another less-restrictive rehab facility approved my case, and I was transferred on the third day. That experience taught me that we can easily begin to think of people as just numbers and cases, but they are real people suffering in the midst of a life-changing event. When dealing with trauma, emotional and mental states are fragile. We must always remember that it is all about relationships, and we must be God's hands extended to all who come across our path.

When we learned that the second rehab facility had accepted me, my husband arranged for me to be transported there. This involved scheduling a Med-Van that could transport me horizontally on a gurney since I could not sit in a wheelchair. We would find out later how very expensive yet necessary this was! He also alerted friends and family of the change in location, and soon a visit schedule was arranged. The second rehab facility was very nice and decorated beautifully to give a sense of calm serenity. The staff were kind and gentle and obviously expert at long-term care of patients. However, when I arrived in my room, I noticed there were *no* monitors to watch my heart and breathing! I was on my own and terrified that something would happen to me during the night and no one would know. The nurses reassured me that they would be checking on me, and I was well enough at this point that I no longer needed heart monitors. While this made me happy, it took a while for me to lose the fear of not being hooked to machines!

There was a TV room with a coffee machine and a computer that my husband would come to use daily. When visitors came, we often went down to this TV room, which afforded more space and didn't look like a bedroom! We soon established a routine of physical therapy and occupational therapy each day, with my husband visiting from 11:00 a.m. until 2:00 p.m. each day to feed me lunch. Even though he had to work second shift and left the rehab facility to go directly to work until after midnight, my husband never missed a day! I waited longingly for the moment he would arrive. If he was late, he had to explain where he was! That is how dependent I had become. He would wheel my bed down the long hallways and out onto the front patio in good weather and feed me lunch outside. I always ordered an extra dessert so he could share in my lunch.

The nurses and caregivers knew him by name and grew to realize that he would advocate for me with a loud voice when needed! When they had trouble locating the Mesna medication that prevented my bladder from bleeding, he persisted until they found a lab across the city that would prepare and ship it. If they were late in bringing medicine or hadn't responded to a request, he questioned them. He was my voice! Each day, he checked to ensure I had gotten my proper medications. I came to depend on his visits for my mental and emotional stability, and he never let me down.

My younger daughter also visited me each and every day. Her support and love were invaluable. She usually came from 4:00 p.m. to 7:00 p.m. and fed me supper. In addition, she would occasionally stop at a drive through and bring me "real people food." Allison proved to be a tremendous counselor and friend, guiding me through my darkest days by describing radical acceptance as a way to deal with pain. She coached and encouraged me as I dealt with waves of depression and despondency from pain and from other medical interventions, and tears would flow. She patiently explained that my feelings were entirely normal and they would pass. She would just sit with me and keep me company, and I treasured that! I gradually learned to deal with pain rather than fight against it because of her help.

My emotions were raw and fragile all the time. I had never been through anything this physically difficult, and many times I felt I was just hanging on by a thread, trying to "stay strong" so I didn't slip down that slippery slope into endless tears. I normally am fairly patient and logical, but all of that goes out the window when you are recovering from a catastrophic illness. Looking back now, I can certainly understand that. But at the time I expected myself to be "normal," so I thought I was just losing my mind! My family and friends were very patient with me.

My daughter usually visited at four every afternoon. One day, there was a severe thunderstorm warning, and the rain started coming down in sheets. The nurses went around to close the blinds because that was the standard protocol in a severe storm. It was four fifteen, then four twenty, and my daughter had not yet arrived. I was absolutely certain that she was in a car wreck because of the rain! She didn't answer her cell phone, and I started crying and could not stop. Two nurses came in to check on me, consoling me and saying, "She is fine. She will be here soon." Because I was still trying to recover *emotionally* from my illness, paralysis, and loss of job, I simply did not have the emotional strength to be logical. I started praying out loud amid the tears. Within another twenty minutes, my daughter arrived, and I was relieved, but I can still remember to this day the sheer terror I felt.

I thoroughly believe that until we experience the deep valley, the dark night of the soul, the desperation, we are unable to identify fully with those who suffer these emotions frequently. After we have been there, it is no longer "sympathy" for someone who is suffering; it is compassionate empathy, realizing that we are all fragile creatures who need a savior. We are all on this journey together. I know that God allowed me to experience this for this reason.

Because I had fears of never being able to return home, Ali told me on a daily basis that I was one day closer to being home. One day, my nurse was going to comb my hair and found a huge tangle in the back where it was falling out. Often when you are just lying in bed as a horizontal patient, your hair never gets combed! She was very kind but said, "Hon, I'm just going to have to cut it out!" The huge tangle also included big clumps of hair that had fallen out in the back because of medication and my constant prone position. It was a mess! I cried and said, "Wait until my daughter comes this afternoon. She'll comb it out." And sure enough, Ali had the patience and persistence to sit behind me with a pick and comb through whatever remained of my hair in the back, taking almost an hour to do so! God blessed me with loving family to help carry me through. My son, Mike, visited also, brought me gifts, and told me to continue to follow doctor's orders and I would be better in no time!

Many friends and coworkers visited while I was in this facility. In October, a holiday called Bosses' Day was always celebrated in my office, and this year they brought the celebration to me in the rehab facility. I received cards, gifts, and money. I received a beautiful devotional book that I use to this day. These made me feel as if I still had a life!

God placed people in my life for a time such as this. Twelve days before I became ill, I met for the first time the mother-in-law of a dear friend, who was a kind and thoughtful Christian lady. Before I became ill, I had given her a CD of Christian music. She very kindly reciprocated by sending to me an iPod shuffle loaded with her favorite Christian music to enjoy with my earbuds in the hospital. Later, this couple would come to visit me in my home. These acts of kindness and mercy enabled me to survive the long and lonely days in the rehab facility. This loving couple helped me financially as well. I will be forever grateful to them!

God was teaching and ministering to me through those songs and through the people and events He was placing in my life. My occupational therapist was a kind woman with whom I became friends. When she worked with me, I would often speak of my faith in God. She then told me that she was a Christian and whispered in my ear that God told her I would make a full recovery. From then on, we prayed together often. One of the aides who I came to love and admire was also a strong Christian, and we often spoke of God's love and protection. I believe that God gave me these people as pillows for me to rest upon during these dark days.

I was told that it would be a long and hard road to recovery, and that was painful to accept. I felt that I was on top of a slope, and the slightest thing could push me over the steep hill going straight down. When I went to my first physical therapy session at this new rehab facility, I could not move my legs at all. The therapist used electrical stimulation, as they had done in the first facility. I was trying so hard to be positive, so I happily told her that I was going to be "walking out of here in no time!" She alerted the chief therapist, who was her supervisor, and I was visited first thing the next morning by this doctor. He was kind but said he wanted me to understand that because of the extent of my muscle myopathy, the recovery process would be very, very slow. (When they tested and recorded my movement, they recorded it as "trace of movement," which means they only could see me trying to contract my muscle—no real movement at all!) After he left my room that morning, I broke down in sobs, not tears, sobs. I thought I would never walk again. At this time, it was September, and I didn't realize that it would take until the next summer for me to be even close to walking again. My husband thought it was cruel of the doctor to tell me that, but he was being realistic, and I had to learn to be realistic as well.

My dear friend encouraged me, often saying, "Stay strong," and his strength became my mantra and my theme, as well as the title of this book. This friend stood by me throughout my recovery in so many ways and truly represented strength in my life. He has been strong for me in many circumstances. Staying strong, for me, became an act of the *will*, a *decision*, and a total leap of *faith*. It was *hard*! But God promised me in his word that He was my strong tower! And I believed with all my heart! Yet the pain and loneliness were very real. I would whisper "Stay strong" to myself, not allowing me to slide down that slippery slope, because that would mean a day of endless tears.

God's Word says, *"I can do all things through Christ which strengthens me"* (Phil. 4:13). Another friend of mine brought me a cross bearing these words, and it is still on my dresser reminding me daily that Christ is my strength. In that hospital room, He became my very real strength as I struggled moment by moment with depression that comes from being trapped in my own, immobile body that would not respond. Each day, I clung to Jesus, who continued to extend that branch to me to hang onto when I felt I was drowning. He never left my side.

More changes were yet to come in my life. In October, I found out that I had lost my job. I spoke to the owner of the company on the phone and asked if I had a job, and she replied that I did not have a job. More loss, devastation, and grief! How could this be happening to me? My job was the fulfillment of all that I found stimulating, exciting, and challenging in my life. I had spent almost half my life there! I had grown with the company from one child care center to eight child care centers. I enjoyed leadership and administration but truly loved going into the classrooms to see the children learning and the babies being cared for. I believed it was God's plan for me to be in this position in the company, where I could freely share his word. I took pleasure in working with, leading, and encouraging people, and in the deep relationships that I had established over the years.

The field of early childhood education was my passion, and I was very knowledgeable and experienced. Why was this being taken from me? I began to feel this was my personal Job story, in which I would lose everything. The loss of my full-time income was devastating to my family, as I was the major breadwinner. The important part was to hang onto God no matter what. He was still sovereign and in control. He knows the plans He has for us! The Bible tells us to give thanks in our troubles because they give us new opportunities to trust Jesus. I definitely felt my trust was being tested and deepened.

This began a new phase of grief and loss for me, as I had poured myself into my job for twenty-six years. Obviously I was still unable to move, still in a rehab facility, and they had made plans to replace me. God once again came to my rescue through my dear, life-saving friends. One friend held a fundraiser on my behalf at his family's restaurant, and another friend raised funds at her child care facility from a parent's night out. Many other friends contributed money, and because of their love and generosity, we were able to pay for my insurance costs through the end of the year as well as many medical costs. I literally don't know how I would have survived if God had not placed these loving people in my life.

On a daily basis, life in the rehab facility became a routine of therapy, medications, and visits from family and friends. I saw small gains in movement when I was able to lift my arm from the elbow up to wave good-bye to my husband, and he took a picture to send our friends! One time in occupational therapy, I was required to pick up all the tiny pieces of a travel-size Connect Four game and drop them into the slots. It was grueling and took me forty-five minutes!

But because of the exercise it gave my hands, the next day I was able to use my fingers to text on my phone! I began to text my daughter who was at home, and she replied "Is someone texting this for you?" I said no, that I had just relearned how to text! That was a major breakthrough and I began to see a very dim light at the end of a long tunnel. Although I could not hold my phone yet, I could touch the screen to send texts, and that brightened my spirit.

Progress was extremely slow with no guarantees for full recovery. If someone could have promised me "After several months of this, you will be as good as new," I believe it would not have been as hard. But there were no such promises! People recovered differently. There was a chance that I would not recover fully. But I had faith and trust in God!

Someone had to help me to do everything while I was in the rehab facility. If I was thirsty, someone had to hold a drink with a straw so I could sip because I couldn't move my hands. If I needed to sit in the wheelchair, I had to be hoisted up in a Hoyer Lift with a canvas sling beneath me hooked up to a machine that would carry me (like a stork!) and place me into the chair. When I wanted to get out of the chair, I had to call someone to put me back in bed. If I was hot, I had to ask for covers to be removed. If I was cold, I could shiver or I could ask for covers to be replaced. If my socks were twisted and bothered my feet, I had to ask someone to fix them. If I had a hair in my eyes, I had to ask someone to remove it. The list goes on—it is endless. There was *nothing* I could do for myself. There are never enough nurses and aides to meet all the needs of the patients, so waiting for help becomes standard. At times it took twenty minutes for someone to come after I hit the call button. Another opportunity to learn patience and trust!

The nurses and aides had to dress and bathe me, and since I could not turn my body, the nurses would have to turn me periodically so I would not put more pressure on the sore on my back. They would turn me to the side and then place pillows behind me to keep me in place. Halfway through the night they would come back and turn me to the other side and place pillows behind me, so I wouldn't put too much pressure on one side. At night, the nurses would help to put my headphones in my ears so I could fall asleep listening to Christian music on my phone. The call button for the nurse was taped to my hand where I could reach it during the night if I needed help, if it didn't fall off! At times when I could not use the call button, I would simply call out "Nurse!" until someone arrived.

I struggled daily with the vulnerability of being paralyzed. Every single thing was a struggle and required assistance—moving the fan, adjusting bed covers, wiping my eyes with a tissue, sipping a drink, eating a meal, changing the TV station, putting socks on and/ or off, turning—I was completely dependent! I came to personally understand the devastation of those who are permanently paralyzed. But I also learned the important life lesson of gratitude! How much we each take for granted daily. I learned to be utterly grateful for any movement of my body and marveled at God's handiwork. Looking back on those days I can see a slow progression toward recovery, but on a daily basis, I felt vulnerable and lost. Again, I leaned heavily on Jesus.

During the two months at this rehab facility, I had to be rushed to the ER at the hospital numerous times. Once, the sore on my back would not stop bleeding after the bandage was changed and the ER doctor had to do a special treatment to stop the bleeding. Another time, I was awakened from a nap and told my heart enzyme levels were high and they thought I might be having a heart attack! I said, "I am fine. I was sound asleep!" But they rushed me to the ER any-way, where I was examined and pronounced to be fine. It was a false reading! The problem was in transporting me—it was no easy car ride! It required moving me from the bed to a gurney by four people holding the sheet below me at the four corners, and hoisting me over to the gurney, hoping I would land well. Then I was transported on the gurney in a Med-Van! When I arrived at the hospital, the same transfer procedure took place. This was always frightening and somewhat painful, but you have very little choice when you are a patient who cannot move!

The rehab facility was told by my insurance company that I would have to leave in the middle of October. I had used all the days allowed in our insurance plan for rehab care. Despite arguments and testimony from doctors, they stuck to their guns. An appeal was submitted in collaboration with my former employer, the insurance agent, and the director of the rehab facility. Formal documentation and statements from the doctors were submitted by all involve. For weeks, I lived on pins and needles, checking every day if we had received an answer, not knowing if I would be staying as I needed to or going home prematurely. Finally, due to a glitch in the interpretation of the length of my stay at the first facility, I was able to appeal and stay in the rehab facility until November 4. Praise God!

Although I wanted desperately to go home, I wanted even more to recover. I was making small steps at progress in my rehab sessions. The thought of going home was enticing and overwhelming at the same time. Again, I felt like I was in the dense forest without a flashlight. What would it be like when I returned home? Who would care for me? I couldn't sit up, dress, or even feed myself? What will we do?

As I looked around at the others in the rehab facility, many were more capable than me. Many could walk and care for themselves with minimum assistance. I began to fight feelings of envy, despair, fear, and depression, wondering if I would ever be able to walk again or care for myself. What did God have in store for me? People assured me that God had saved me for a reason—that He wasn't done with me yet!! But what would my future hold? Would I ever fully recover?

CHAPTER 5

Caring for Mama

*Call to me and I will answer you, and show you great
and mighty things which you do not know.*
—Jeremiah 32:2–3

One advantage (if you want to call it that) to being paralyzed for a year is that you have lots of time to reflect on your life. No one would choose a situation such as this and I am certainly not making light of it. I also lost significant weight during my illness, but I would not recommend it as a diet plan! But when we are forcibly removed from the hectic treadmill of life, we have an opportunity to evaluate everything in the context of a stark new reality. Although frightening, it is also enlightening. I realized that God had his mighty hand on me throughout my life, and was preparing me in baby steps for what was to come. Later I would realize that while this became clear as I looked at my past, it would also provide me with the *hope* I desperately needed to move forward into the future. He will always be there for me!

As mentioned earlier, my childhood was a happy time, with loving parents and good friends. The fifties and sixties were a time in America dedicated to strong family values, with TV shows like *Ozzie and Harriet, Leave it to Beaver,* and *Father Knows Best* portraying the idyllic home in the suburbs with the white picket fence, mom in the kitchen, father at the office, and two perfect children. My family was a happy one, even though we did not fit this mold completely. My mom and dad were forty-six and forty-seven when I was born, which was much older than the norm at that time. My mom did stay home, and my dad was a steelworker. My mom did not drive. Our neighborhood was very blue collar and was anchored by our Catholic church to which we walked for Sunday Mass. My mom often attended daily Mass, and I went to the church elementary school, and later Catholic high school, and a Jesuit University. The surrounding neighbors were primarily Slovak and Hungarian, and Slovak was my parent's first language although English was spoken in our home. I grew up longing to be American in every way!

In 1976, tragedy struck our family when my forty-one-year-old brother-in-law dropped dead on a business trip, leaving my thirty-two-year-old sister widowed with three young children. Three months later, my dad died suddenly at the age of seventy. He died five months before I was to be married. My family rallied around each other to survive these losses, and we became very close. We were not wealthy, and we were not handed anything on a silver platter. We learned the importance of hard work and sticking together. These life lessons would carry us all the way through and provide a resource to me as I dealt with my devastating illness. Jesus had brought me so far He would not abandon me now.

My sister eventually remarried a wonderful man with three children of his own to raise. They became a real-life version of *The Brady Bunch*, only real-life rarely matches the TV portrayal. For many years, they dealt with the trials as well as the joys of a blended family with six teenagers and one bathroom! Fortunately, as they turned to God, He provided the guidance and wisdom to raise a healthy, productive family.

My husband and I had met in college, where I was the first in my family to graduate with a four-year degree. We married at the age of twenty-three and bought our own house in the suburbs, where two little girls were born in quick succession. Fast forward to the age of thirty, when my mother was diagnosed with Alzheimer's disease. This is a tragic diagnosis for any family, and even more so for us, after all that we had endured. When I was thirty and my girls were three and one, I took my mother into my home to live with us.

My husband had a great job as a salesman for a machine tool company and was transferred to the Toledo area to assume a new territory of his own. What a great promotion! Unfortunately, it meant moving away from our small, close family to a brand-new environment. While my husband began working in his new territory during the week and coming home only on weekends, I stayed back in our home with my two baby girls and my sick mom to sell our home. Somehow the Lord carried me through this phase!

Our house had a lock box to enable realtors to show the home when I was not there. One time, I was in the shower and did not hear the knocking of a realtor who had brought a young couple to see our home. I came into the kitchen in a bathrobe and towel with my two little girls, only to find a realtor and two prospective buyers standing in my kitchen! They apologized profusely and quickly left. The home was sold by the end of the summer, and we were able to move to Toledo to join my husband.

My mother's struggle with Alzheimer's disease was unfamiliar territory to our family. Although I loved my mother intensely and believed I could care for her in my home until the end, it proved to be too much for our family. The course of Alzheimer's disease can be cruel as you lose your loved one a little bit more each day. For a long time, I was able to take Mom to an adult-care facility for the day two days per week for mental stimulation that would slow the course of the disease, but it proved relentless. All too soon, she did not know where she was or who we were and became paranoid and frightened. She began to hallucinate and thought people (who were not there) were ignoring her. This broke my heart, as my mom and I had been best friends! We had to admit her to a nursing home. We traveled the road of the very long good-bye of Alzheimer's disease.

For a young woman of thirty with two babies age three and one, caring for a mom with Alzheimer's was a lot to handle. On top of that, my husband was gone during the week and came home on weekends, and I had stayed home to sell the house and pack to move out of town. It could only have been God carrying me through this turbulent time. My girls and I often speak of visiting Grandma and having dinner with her, as I took my daughters to visit her often while she was in a care facility. Although they were very young, the experience was a life lesson for all of us about the blessing of family!

As I looked back on that time, I was comforted and encouraged that once again, Jesus carried me through! Again, I could see the hand of God holding me up during everyday trials, and giving me strength to overcome. I gained wisdom and hope from remembering these things as I faced the long road ahead of me. As God led me through these memories, I saw the tapestry of my life unfolding and took great courage that He would indeed show me many things that I did not know. He was sovereign and ever faithful, and I was not alone.

Much of the scenario in my mother's life and how it impacted me was repeated in my own life. I became so ill that my children had to care for me. My life had come full circle. As I reflected on the "river of time," I had great peace knowing that God cares for us through all stages of our lives. As I had cared for my mother, my children cared for me.

What I did not fully realize during the time that I cared for my mom was that my young girls were watching! Even if they did not fully realize what was happening, they perceived that Grandma lived at our house, and we cared for her. I had no way of knowing at that time that this would come full circle in my family's life—there would be a time that my children would care for me. God was showing me as I recovered that my whole life had been preparation for what I was going through at the present time.

CHAPTER 6

Coming Home

You, Lord, give perfect peace to those who keep their
purpose firm and put their trust in you.
—Isaiah 26:3

The whole time I was in the rehab nursing home, I dreamed about going home—about being in my family room, sitting on the couch in my pajamas, in front of the fireplace, with my legs curled under me, sipping hot chocolate. Just picturing myself doing that brought me peace and joy. Little did I realize that it would take me over a year to achieve that goal!

The morning of November 4, 2014, dawned as a crisp, early autumn day. Leaves were changing color and pumpkins were everywhere. Inside my world in the nursing home, the day had finally arrived for me to return home. It had been almost four months since the day I was taken to the ER with a cough and put on life support and woke up paralyzed. It was a long journey thus far, but this was truly just the beginning.

Preparations were started for me to return home. First order of business was for the stomach tube, or "peg," to be removed. It could only be removed by the doctor who inserted it. Therefore, a Med-Van transport was ordered for me, and I was placed on the gurney to take me to the vehicle. As I was wheeled down the hallway, I rejoiced that this was the second last day I would ride down this hallway. The next day would mark my trip home at long last. I was wheeled into the Med-Van and taken to the doctor's office, my husband riding along with me. I was still emotionally fragile and fearful of many things, and Ryan was always at my side. They took me into the doctor's office, and we waited nervously. I didn't know what to expect. I just knew that this tube was sticking right out of my stomach and it had to go!!

All the other medical devices—ventilator, IV lines, heart monitor, blood-oxygen monitor—had been removed, and this "thing" was the last to go. I recalled the many times this stomach feeding tube was used—almost daily! When it was time for my medication, the nurses would crush and mix my many pills into a thick, bitter concoction that was diluted with warm water and fed through the stomach tube. It went directly into my stomach, so when the mixture was poured, it felt the warm water trickling through my stomach. It was always a strange experience thinking someone was pouring something directly into your stomach. But I was unable to swallow the myriad of pills, so this was the much easier choice. What would I do when I went home?

The doctor finally came in and pulled out the stomach tube with no anesthetic, assuring me it would not hurt. Although it was a bit of a shock and sounded like a *pop*, it was not painful! I would no longer have a stomach tube! Another milestone for me. A simple bandage covered the area, and I was good to go! It would take about two weeks for this area to fully close, but it never caused any pain. Isn't God amazing? This experience showed me a whole new side of medicine, and life, that I never knew existed!

Several multidisciplinary meetings with the medical team, my husband, and myself took place at the nursing home to discuss how I would be cared for at home, how I would be transported home, how I would be transported to the subsequent doctor visits, how my medications would be obtained, who to contact in case of an emergency, which nursing company would assist us going forward. Multiple papers had to be signed by my husband, and we received discharge papers and a long list of instructions. Finally, the day of my long-awaited departure arrived. Throughout the day, nurses, aides, and therapists who had worked with me during my two month stay came to visit. The director of the facility came to wish me well, as she had been closely involved in my case. She advocated on my behalf when I was in danger of losing my insurance and my bed in the nursing home. Through her efforts and others, I was approved to stay an additional month.

Some staff members were emotional, and all wished me continued success. One occupational therapist cried and said, "If I only had two more months, I know I could get your hands and arms to work!" I was touched by that, and also encouraged that she saw that in my future. One of the hardest parts of being paralyzed was that there were no solid guarantees that I would ever recover or how much I would recover. I prayed daily for full recovery, but when it was so slow in coming, I wasn't certain of my fate.

A Med-Van was called to take me home, and we again had to repeat the procedure with transferring me to the gurney. This time I felt more assured, knowing I would be going home. Nothing sounded so good to me as the word *home*. When the transport arrived and I was transferred to the gurney, I was taken down the hallway for my very last trip. The feelings were overwhelming. I was finally, actually going home. The fears of never seeing my home again had been vanquished. As I was pushed down the hall, I said good-bye to everyone, and they waved and offered best wishes. This would be the last time I would go down this hallway, and I was grateful and overjoyed. I was moved with emotion and gratitude for all the nurses and aides who

God had appointed to care for me during this difficult time, and I prayed for them all.

When the van brought me home for the first time, the sounds and sights of my foyer, kitchen, and family room were a balm for my soul. Wood flooring had just been installed in the foyer, so I was able to see that for the first time—beautiful! There is truly no feeling like coming home again after a long time away. God was blessing me with this very special joy! But again, I had no perspective on how long it would take for me to return to "normal." I didn't realize then that I would literally live in one room, my family room, for the next year of my life! Normal again was my goal, but it was a long way off!

A hospital bed had been set up in my family room, with an air mattress that was inflated by a motor attached to the bed. This was to provide a soft cushion for the sore on my back. A small Hoyer lift had been delivered from the medical supply company, as well as a large reclining wheelchair. Because my muscles were still too weak to support me sitting upright, I had to sit at a forty-five-degree angle, with pillows supporting me on either side and under my arms.

It took several days before I was able to adjust to sitting the "big" wheelchair. The first time my family attempted to use the Hoyer lift to move me from the bed into the wheelchair, we were all nervous. It was trial and error for sure; the problem was that I was swinging suspended in the air and there was not much room for error. Everyone was nervous. Although the procedure became easier over time, none of us completely lost our nervousness.

The first attempt at sitting in the wheelchair was doomed to failure. My husband got me lifted up into the air properly, manually pushed over to the wheelchair properly, but when he lowered me into the chair I promptly slid right out! Because I could not control my sliding, I was screaming and saying, "Help! Help me!" My poor family together grabbed under my arms and pulled me back up into the chair. Keeping in mind that I had a pressure sore on my back, this was not a fun experience! I declared the chair unfit for me and refused to try it again! We called the medical supply company and told them to pick it up and bring me something better.

Luckily, the physical therapy supervisor paid me a visit the very next day. She suggested that we put a blanket in the chair to make it less slippery. She supervised as my family used the Hoyer lift to carry me and place me into the chair. She showed them how to adjust my position by lifting under my arms and pulling the canvas from behind to make me sit taller in the chair so I wouldn't slide. Since my arms just dropped down to the side when they were unsupported and I could not lift them back up, bed pillows were placed under each arm for support. The footrest of the big wheelchair was extended, and pillows were placed under each of my legs to keep them in place. Only then could I be pushed up the metal ramp, purchased for this reason, to raise me up from the family room into the kitchen.

There was a tremendous learning curve for my family, who were now my caregivers. My older daughter had returned to Tennessee by this time, as she was attending college. She would return at the Thanksgiving break. My younger daughter, my husband, and my son had to learn how to use the lift once I was able to be placed in the wheelchair. This involved turning me to my side, placing a canvas sling under me, then wheeling the lift over to the bed until it was over me. The canvas sling had hooks that attached to the top of the lift, then the handle had to be cranked until the lift moved me up into the air (like a stork). Then the lift was pushed over to where I was to be placed, such as the wheelchair or the couch, lowered, and released. Sometimes it would catch on the carpet and almost tip over, which would have meant an emergency call to 911. The canvas sling would remain under me until it was time to move again.

Since I was still unable to move in any way, if I was placed too low or on the side, I would have to be adjusted by pulling the canvas sling. After a few adjustments, we would get it right. I couldn't help;

I could only describe if I was uncomfortable. My family patiently worked to make me comfortable. It was marvelous to be out of the bed in a sitting position, but it was also exhausting. My core muscles worked hard to support me but after about two hours, I had to get out of the wheelchair. The Hoyer lift would again be used, and I would be placed back in a prone position in my bed. These were exhausting procedures for my family as well.

I marveled at how skilled the therapists are. My family was in a quandary of confusion, not knowing how to deal with this new reality. With the guidance and support of therapists, we were finding our way through the forest. My family had to repeat this lengthy and difficult procedure each and every day from November until April, and it was exhausting. My husband and my daughters would take turns "moving Mom." I would be moved to the chair or to the couch, and so I would have to be moved back to the bed. Sometimes, this was twice per day. These are some of the unseen burdens on families dealing with disability or illness. It was physically strenuous and emotionally devastating to a family who is dealing with so many other issues at the same time. I am so blessed that they cared enough to do this difficult work to keep me going through this time.

My family was responsible for my medications and daily routine. When I first came home, I was still not able to feed myself. It took me four weeks to learn to eat alone. My husband and my younger daughter suddenly had to take the place of a staff of nurses and aides in the nursing home. My daughter lived there and worked at home, but my husband had to keep his job since he was now the only breadwinner with insurance! We developed a routine where my daughter gave my first round of medication and breakfast at 7:00 a.m., then took a nap. My husband was still asleep at this time as he comes home from work at 12:30 a.m. every day. He would then wake up a little later to see if I needed anything. Everyone was afraid to let me sleep downstairs in the family room all alone, so my dear husband slept in the recliner beside me every night for a year! Around 10:00 a.m., he would use the Hoyer and put me in the wheelchair for a while. Then my daughter would prepare lunch and feed it to me. I would go back into the bed after lunch.

Soon my physical and occupational therapy sessions at home began. The outlook was very dismal at first, as I could not do anything, even squeeze their hand, but my therapists were cheerful and encouraging. My physical therapist came three times per week for one hour, and my occupational therapist came three times per week for one hour. They were steadfast and faithful, even coming to the house when it was 14 below zero degrees outside! I came to look forward to seeing them and was eager to show that I had made progress. They were kind to notice the slightest amount of change, even if I could reach a little farther or move my muscles a little more. They were strong for me when I was not strong. Even though they also were not certain I would recover fully, they kept encouraging me in a calm, determined way.

Physical therapy at this point is not what anyone would imagine. To be able to lift my arm, to be able to move my feet, and perhaps move my leg a little was an accomplishment. My therapist frequently told me that he was proud of how hard I was trying. I wondered what he meant, thinking anyone would naturally work hard to regain their strength. However, he told me of patients that he had who would not cooperate. One older man said he was just "too tired" and would not get off the bed, wouldn't even sit up. Finally, my therapist told him, "If you do not cooperate, I am not coming back." So the man cooperated. But I also prayed for those who were so discouraged and had given up hope of any recovery. My physical therapist told me, "I am doing for you what I would want someone to do for me—get me back to normal!" That is exactly what I wanted. That same therapist who wasn't exactly sure how he would do it at first would later tell others that I was his greatest success story. Their encouragement made me stronger each day.

During this time the cards, letters, and gifts kept coming from friends and relatives. Some contained gifts of money, which were very much needed and appreciated (see picture). Those thoughts, prayers, and wishes kept me going through a very dark and cold winter. One friend said, "You have many good years ahead of you in early childhood education." Later I would have a dream involving this person. I was at the top of a tall staircase on the second floor in a bright white room with many windows and high ceiling. I stood next to a man dressed all in white. My friend came in the door with eight kids, all three-year-olds, to learn karate in a classroom on the first floor. One child cried and said he couldn't do the exercises because he couldn't move. I "floated" down the staircase and helped the child. I told him he would be okay because I will be there to help him. He said, "I can't do it because I have a trach!" I looked at him and said, "Look, I have a trach too!" He hugged me and tried the exercises again. His father was grateful and thanked me for helping him. I think often of that dream.

Other cards and gifts kept coming. My cousin told me in a card, "We are as strong as our parents were." I remember to this day how my spirit lifted through these encouraging words and remembered that God tells us in His Word, *"Let no corrupting talk come out of your mouths, but only such as is good for building up, as fits the occasion, that it may give grace to those who hear"* (Eph. 4:29). I thank God for giving me these good people who offered encouraging words, and who continually built me up when I needed it most. This is another way Jesus was carrying me through my dark night.

When I arrived home on November 4, it was three days from my birthday. When my birthday arrived, I had visits and gifts from friends and a birthday dinner cooked by my daughter. My goal at the nursing home was to be home by my birthday, and I reached that goal! This would be one of many milestones I would reach with the help of God.

Since it was November, and the weather in Ohio was getting much cooler, we had to determine how I would stay warm since my bed was located in the southwestern corner of the room near a brick wall, and I often felt cold. We purchased a room space heater, which worked well but eventually caused the electricity to overload and short! That was not our only calamity that winter. Our area of the city had the gas shut off at the main pipes for a period of time. Since we have a gas furnace, and my husband was already at work, I called the gas company and explained that I was disabled and could not move. Also, I could only be transported in a Med-Van since I was not able to sit in a chair! If the furnace stopped working that night, I could very well freeze. They sent someone to the house to fix it within forty-five minutes.

Because the winter was so very cold that year, our water pipes froze in our upstairs bathroom, water would not drain from the tub, and water leaked through the kitchen ceiling. Our son-in-law and older daughter were visiting for Thanksgiving, so he was able to help unfreeze the pipes so we could use the bathtub. At one point we were dealing with so many issues that we didn't know which problem to solve first. It was not enough that I was paralyzed and family life revolved around "caring for Mom." It was as if Satan was saying "So you think you've got this, huh? Well, try getting through *this*!" We never gave up hope! At times we laughed because we were all just trying to do the best we could and hang onto our sanity. God always came through—He never let us down! Through it all, God provided family and friends to back us up, and to help us get through the hard times.

Each month, I kept thinking and hoping that "maybe next month I'll be able to sit up alone, to stand, to walk," but as the months slowly continued, progress was very slow and hard to see. The time before Christmas was busy as I tried to help hang ornaments on the tree (if they were at chair height) and succeeded in hanging about five ornaments that my daughter handed me one by one!

Christmas was fast approaching with all the joy that the season brings. It is my favorite holiday as it celebrates the birth of our Savior, but also the Holy Family. I have collected Nativity scenes for many years and have about forty of various sizes and shapes. We enjoy displaying the Nativity scenes each year and recollecting where we purchased them or who gave them to us. It was especially poignant to me this year, as God's divine plan for loving families was being played out within my home. God intended for family life to be central to human existence as a way to protect, nurture, and guide children and parents alike. I was experiencing the beauty of family just as the Holy Family did on that precious night so long ago. Jesus was born into a family who would care for and nurture him, as my family cared for and nurtured me. The celebration of the Holy Family became very real to me that year. As my daughter put them out that year, I was overwhelmed with gratitude to God that I was able to survive to see another Christmas season with my beloved family. But the road was still very long.

My 60th birthday, 11/7/2013

Katie and I, 7/4/2014, 6 days before I collapsed

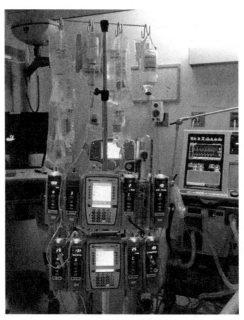

Machines in ICU keeping me alive

Waking from coma 7/30/14

In hospital 8/5/2014

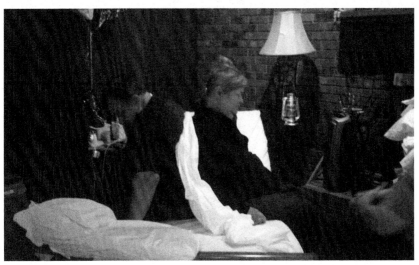

Physical Therapy at home 11/14/14

Sitting in wheelchair at table 3/15/15

Sitting on front porch 4/21/15

Belinda and I in Atlanta 10/15/15

December, 2016

Fundraiser by dear friends 11/14

Gifts from Ravens Organization

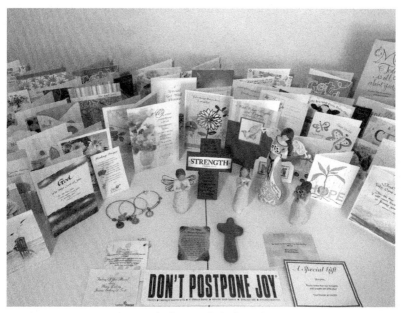
Cards from adult friends

Cards from children in my child care center

CHAPTER 7

Long Road to Recovery

But they who wait upon the Lord shall renew their strength;
they shall mount up with wings like eagles; they shall run
and not be weary; they shall walk and not faint.
—Isaiah 40: 31

"Come on, try one more time!"

I strained my muscles as hard as I could to make my leg move, even just a little.

"I know you can do it! Just one more!"

I tried to oblige my physical therapist with every ounce of strength I had. You would think I was training for the Olympics! All I was being asked to do is to move my leg ever so slightly to the side while remaining motionless on my hospital bed. When my left leg budged half an inch, my therapist shouted, "Yes! I knew you could do it!"

This was how my physical therapy sessions would proceed, three days per week for an hour. Steve and I became quite good friends, as he could see how hard I was trying even though nothing was happening! He came with a variety of tasks for me to perform, and he never gave up hope. Because he believed in me, I could believe in myself. God had chosen the exact right person to be my therapist.

Our Christmas holiday was over, but it had been very beautiful and special, even though I could only sit in the reclining wheelchair for a short period of time. My daughter and her husband came from Tennessee to celebrate with us, and my family prepared a holiday feast without my help. They managed to position me in my reclining wheelchair at the dining room table, and my heart was overflowing with joy and gratitude that I could be here for another Christmas. I carefully moved a tablespoon from plate to mouth, spilling just a little, as I managed to finish my delicious Christmas feast prepared by my two daughters.

I had also received a very encouraging e-mail from the pastor who prayed over me when I was in a coma. He told me that God shared with him that I was to tell my story as a witness to the power and glory of God! He said he was not free to share that word from God with me until this time. He also said that my life was taking a new turn, and he gave me the verse Isaiah 60 and 61: *"Arise, shine, for your light has come, and the glory of the Lord rises upon you... The Spirit of the sovereign Lord is upon me because the Lord has anointed me to proclaim good news to the poor."* He told me I was a living miracle and that God was going to use my story. I was thrilled! He also told me that I would not be long in bed and that I should start recording my thoughts and impressions.

Finally, I began to feel that something was making sense. The Lord was speaking through this pastor to encourage me and offer me the promise that I had a future. I was faced with the prospect of the cold winter months, and very slow progress in my recovery. In my heart, I believed that if I could recover my movement, my life would return to my pre-illness normal. I would learn later that this could never be. God was beginning to show me that my life might change, that it would have meaning, and that my story might help others in a similar situation. Unfortunately, the roller coaster continued.

As with all families where many lives intersect, other stories and dramas were unfolding simultaneously. The dramatic events surrounding my illness reverberated within my family like ripples on a quiet pond. My daughter in Tennessee had gone home after Christmas to resume her studies at University of Tennessee and live with her husband. But the burden of my daily care became too great for my husband, son, and younger daughter to manage on their own. My husband and son worked all day, and my younger daughter was left to care for me day and night. Physically, emotionally, and mentally, exhaustion set in. We could not go on like this. We were faced with putting me back into a nursing home, which insurance would not cover; hiring help at home, which insurance would not cover; or having my older daughter return to assist in my care until I was ambulatory.

After many prayer, tears, and phone calls, Jen decided to return from Tennessee from January until May, taking her college classes online. She had to jump through many hoops to do so because her classes were not online classes. Her professors simply agreed to do this for her since she was an excellent student and this was a family medical emergency. Jen was able to stay in Toledo and share in the burden of caring for an invalid Mom as she continued her studies. Praise God that He gave Jen the heart and will to do so. Later Jen would tell me, "Mom, that's what families do!" I will forever be grateful for her selfless offer to care for me.

Jen's husband, Alan, was tremendously supportive as well. He had been through a lot, including a bad fall resulting in partial paralysis and had willed himself to regain mobility, so he knew what I was going through. Although he stayed in Tennessee to continue working, he visited several times to help out. Once in February, he walked through the door and immediately said to me, "I have been praying about this, and I know you have the strength to do this. You will walk again!" At a time when I doubted myself, when I was depressed, when the days dragged on with no perceptible change, when I was tired and discouraged, God used Alan to tell me that He was still there—He had not abandoned me and I would be okay. Jen would stay until May when I was a little more capable and could do a little more for myself.

I had come to the point where I could now feed myself, which was a huge relief to my family. One less chore to do for Mom. However, I could not write in any way. I could not make my fingers bend to hold a pen or pencil. The myopathy had seriously affected my right hand more than my left, and my right hand needed extensive occupational therapy. I could not open the hand fully. This would be a very long time coming. Therefore, If I were to record my thoughts, I would at least need to have a laptop. I mentioned this to a dear friend, hoping I could buy one through his connection. This friend sent over a laptop for me at no cost! He said, "You will not see a bill." This dear friend has been beside me every step of the way and has been a huge encouragement in the writing of my story. God was so good, and again, providing all my need through his outstretched hands of my dearest friends! My new laptop arrived loaded with software, and I made a valiant attempt to use it in those early days. The first entry in my journal is dated January 2015. It is this same laptop computer that has allowed me to share my story with you.

Also in January, the Ravens won a NFL playoff game against the Steelers, and my friend with family members who are part of the Ravens Organization was able to obtain a "Faith and Guts" shirt for me! This is a shirt that the team members wore (see picture). The Ravens Organization provides a model for the impact that high-profile people can have on the rest of us in a very positive way. They are not only a dynamic NFL team, they are people who honor God in their daily life. I have great admiration for the them. These awesome, supportive people have become supportive friends and prayer warriors for me. God was caring for me in every way!

I learned that OJ Brigance, who played for the Ravens, had contracted ALS and could no longer play but was retained by the Ravens Organization as a spiritual advisor. I read his book called *Strength of a Champion*, and it spoke to me immediately. His deep spiritual insights encouraged me as they had encouraged his fellow team members. He handled his devastating, progressive illness with courage, grace, and strength. I read in his book that "adversity introduces us to ourselves." That was a powerful statement for me to accept. I learned from him and determined that I would also lean on God's strength and grace to get me through. I later e-mailed OJ and was thrilled to receive an e-mail in return, telling me that he was praying for me! This truly became an emotional turning point in my recovery. It also told me clearly that God reaches out to his children through the testimony of other believers. Words of encouragement are God's hands extended to his people.

Intensive physical therapy comprised the next several months. Going through this time was grueling, but looking back, it is quite amazing to see the progress that was made. God has created a miraculous mechanism for regeneration and healing in the human body. My muscles were completely atrophied during my illness. My calf muscle looked like a flabby arm muscle swaying in the wind! It was shocking how weak and lifeless I had become. However, I had been told that once my body was ready, my muscles would respond. Although it was hard for me to see at the time, this was happening.

Steve was determined for me to sit on the side of my bed—a huge feat! My husband sat on the other side so we could be back-to-back for my support. Steve helped me swing my legs over the side, and then pulled me by my arms into an upright position. Then they helped me to sit up, and when I did, I felt like a roly-poly doll. My husband sat firmly with his back against mine as a backrest. (see picture) I could not sit up straight. Push my shoulder and I went down and couldn't get up. Thank goodness for laughter because we sure needed it. I gradually gained a bit of strength and could sit on the side of the bed without toppling over.

Then Steve began the Tupperware tumbler game. He would hold out a stack of tumblers and I would have to lean over, grab one, and put it in his other hand. At first, the tumblers were close, but as I got better, he held them farther and farther away from me. I was sitting on the side of the bed, and I had to reach way out to get those suckers. He laughed and kind of enjoyed my misery. Sounds easy? Try it if your core muscles are like Jell-O. I would fall over, and he would just laugh and help me back up. We continued this for three months, three times per week. Who said paralysis isn't fun?

After I was sitting better on the side of the bed, Steve started making me lie back down all by myself. Easy, huh? Hardly! I could lie back in the bed, but I couldn't get my legs up. I had to practice raising one leg and then the other into the bed. This took *two* months. I also eventually had to learn to get myself out of the bed. This took lots of practice as well. I was taught to turn on my left side, try to pull my arm under me and put my elbow on the bed, then try to raise myself up just a little. By hanging onto the bars beside my bed with my opposite right hand, I could theoretically pull and push myself up into a sitting position. This was one of the hardest things I had to accomplish—sitting up in bed. But eventually I mastered it.

At the end of January, the day came to try standing with a walker. I first had to practice by pushing my feet on the floor to exercise my thighs! That is all I did for a week, and it was exhausting. Finally, the time came. I was extremely nervous. Part of me feared that I would fail and disappoint everyone, including myself. I sat on the side of the bed, grabbed the walker, and Steve and my husband each held me under the arms. One, two, three, they lifted me to a standing position as I hung onto the walker for dear life. My legs were wobbly, my back hunched over, my head down, but I could stand for ten seconds with them holding me. And then I collapsed on the bed. How the heck would I ever walk again?

This exercise continued through February and March and got a little bit better beginning in April. It was very difficult. I prayed continually for strength. As Charles Spurgeon said, "Pray so that every breath is a prayer." It was a natural to me as breathing! I had to will myself to do the exercises even when I was dog-tired and did not want to do them—because this was the only way back! Eventually, I would be able to stand holding onto the walker for one full minute without them holding me. Now that is progress. Hard-fought and long in coming, but progress.

My feelings were all over the board during these months, and that was hard to bear. I learned through prayer that I could not depend on my feelings! They are fleeting and not tied to any kind of foundation—sometimes on top of the world, and sometimes in the pit of despair. His word tells us, *"Trust in the Lord with all your heart and lean not on your own understanding; in all your ways submit to him, and he will make your paths straight"* (Prov. 3:6). Until I was imprisoned in a body that didn't work, totally dependent on those around me, without a certain future, without a job, I was not able to fully appreciate those words. When all is lost, when the future is dim, when you are not in control, when your feelings change from moment to moment, *lean not on your own understanding*. Lean only and completely on GOD. He is the one who will never forsake or leave you. Surrender and submit it *all* to Him, and He will come through.

One morning, God placed the word *determined* in my mind. Out of the blue, as if it was written on a chalkboard, there it was, *determined*. It was a very distinct message from God, and I knew He was telling me I must be determined if I was to succeed. From that point on, I repeated the word determined as I performed each exercise, with my therapist or on my own. Just saying that word gave me the mental resolve to do it. My dear friend would also text me occasionally to see how I was doing, and he never failed to say, "Stay Strong!" These became my buzzwords back to mobility. I was *determined* to stay strong!

I continued to use my laptop to record in my journal and that proved to be very therapeutic for me. By the end of February I was able to stand with my walker with the help of Steve, and I was able to transition to the smaller, normal wheelchair. This was much easier for me to learn to push around the house once my arms were strong enough. To practice standing, Steve pushed me to the kitchen sink and had me stand up from the wheelchair holding onto the sink. When standing and holding the sink, I had to do "knee bends." If I could go down an inch, he was thrilled. One day, I was a bit too confident and tried to do a deep knee bend but couldn't get back up. I started to fall backward, and Steve caught me and guided me back into the wheelchair. So much for changing up my routine.

My exercises were changing and becoming more difficult as I grew stronger. I was learning to roll to one side and then to the other to build my core muscles. I was attempting to raise my knees up while lying on my back. I tried so hard at this one that my friend wrote a prayer for me:

> *We come to you in the name of King Jesus! We come to you in agreement asking that the Holy Spirit would bring to mind the things you want us to pray for! Father in Jesus name I come before you that you would by the power of the Holy Spirit bring LIFE into Mary Ann's legs—and back— and feet—and arms—from the top of her head to the soles of her feet bring STRENGTH—let her do today what she could not do yesterday!! Each day doing more than the day before! Holy Spirit*

set Mary Ann's mind under your control—let her see herself walking soon—give her a vision of this! Always Father we want to be open to your leading and learn from you! Keep us pliable before you! Thank you! In Jesus name our savior and King! Amen."

She and I prayed this prayer together in agreement each day beginning on April 2, and within one month, I was able to walk with a walker. God is good!

Although the daily grind from January until April seemed like a life sentence, in April I was able to start standing a bit with a walker. Steve and Ryan had me stand with the walker beside my bed, and Steve explained that he wanted me to just lift my feet and move them step by step to the right. I followed his instructions, and with all the strength I had, I moved my feet to the right. I took three steps. We were all overjoyed! It felt like this would actually happen one day. God was showing me that He was faithful in his part, but I must be faithful in my part. It would have been much easier if I had been guaranteed that I would have full recovery, but in medicine, there is no guarantee. God was encouraging me through the people and events in my life, and slowly I saw changes. I worked hard physically as well as emotionally and spiritually. My dear friends kept encouraging me to stay strong, and that motivated me to do it for them. I tried to write in my laptop journal as often as possible, which was easier as my smaller wheelchair could be pushed to the kitchen table.

The Lord was speaking to me throughout this time. I prayed his word several times per day, and kept all my scriptures and a prayer journal on my phone, which was always beside me. It helped me when I was feeling down to immediately turn to scripture verses, and let his word just soak through me. My situation stayed the same, but His spirit in me gave me strength and assurance that I was not alone.

Jesus told *me "Thy word is a lamp to my feet, and a light to my path"* (Ps. 119:105). He was talking about *my* feet! I would need a *lamp* to my *feet* because I would be walking again. He surprised me many times by giving me insight into words that brought me *hope* for my journey.

My occupational therapist came three times per week for an hour each time. At first I was resistant to the use of tools she brought to help me, such as the stick to help with putting on socks or the grabber to pick things up from the floor. January through March, I was primarily in a prone position in bed, so Sue taught me how to get my shirt and pants on lying down. When she first taught me what to do, I secretly thought, *I will never be able to do this!* I couldn't lift my arms; I couldn't reach my feet. But God reminded me of my word, *determined.* I became determined to get my shirt over my head. Try to do that when you cannot lift your arms. It made for many laughable moments with my head buried in my shirt, unable to extricate myself. Sue would patiently wait until I could free myself on my own. I learned to do some things as well. I learned to get my arm into a shirt and then throw it over my head. Hopefully, it landed in the right place. Fortunately, she was very patient with me.

As I was learning from PT to stand with a walker, I was also learning from OT how to "scootch" into my wheelchair. Sue placed a special, smooth board onto the wheelchair and the side of the bed. I had to sit and move close to the board and scootch my bottom onto the board and keep scootching until I got into the wheelchair. Success! With someone helping to hold the board, I was able to get myself into my wheelchair. My core muscles became so strong from this scootching that within a week, I was able to stand with the walker, pivot, and sit down in the wheelchair. No more board! Progress! Healing!

Sue also taught me to become more useful in the kitchen, which was helpful for my family. I learned to push my wheelchair to the dishwasher and unload it onto the counter. I learned to wash the front of the refrigerator. I learned to get my own drink. Eventually, I could stand holding onto the counter and actually put dishes into the cabinets, one by one. I had many exercises to do with my hands and arms with progressively heavier weights. After much work, I eventually got to lift a five pound weight over my head with a straight arm ten times. Progress! Healing!

Because I often felt useless in my own home, I tried to help out wherever I could with kitchen work. I even tried to bake cookies! My family favorite are Ritz cookies, which are Ritz cracker sandwiches with peanut butter dipped into melted chocolate. Easy? Not when you are recovering from paralysis! My daughter brought me a small bowl of peanut butter and some crackers on a tray as I sat in my wheelchair. I made the peanut butter cracker sandwiches, then she brought the melted chocolate, and I used a fork to dip them. What a mess! More chocolate got on the tray and on me than anywhere, but again I was determined! When I could make ten cookies, I considered it a success. Baby steps of progress!

Many tasks we take for granted had to be performed for me because I simply was not able to do them. For instance, my daughter had to shampoo my hair at the kitchen sink while I sat in the wheelchair. Afterward, she combed and dried my hair. She also had to bring my toothbrush and toothpaste to my bed so I could brush my teeth. At the beginning of my illness, I went for many months without having my teeth brushed! Needless to say, I became a toothbrushing fanatic once I could do this for myself. But my daughter had to bring me the brush, etc. I could do virtually nothing without bothering someone else for help.

As if the paralysis and pain were not enough, the chemotherapy drug I took for six months caused me to lose my hair. Because I was in bed lying on my back so much of the day, the hair loss was primarily in the back of my head. I never looked in a mirror so I didn't know the extent of it. The front of my hair looked fairly normal, but the back was completely bald! When visitors would come, my girls would tell me "Now mom, just don't turn your head from side to side. Keep your head still." I am glad I didn't have access to a mirror very often, because that would be one more loss to deal with.

My hair stylist and I are friends, as I have been trusting her with my hair for over 15 years. I have followed her all around town as she moved to different salons and finally opened her own, as she knows me and my hair very well. Because we have such a long professional relationship, she was extremely supportive and told my daughter that when I was ready, she would come to my house to do my hair. Early on I was contemplating purchasing a wig, but decided to wait. My stylist gave my daughter special products to use with my hair to encourage growth, and they were useful. It would be ten full months before my daughter took me to the salon for my first haircut, which was another huge milestone. My stylist cut and styled my hair for free for several months, and knew exactly how to handle hair that was fragile because of chemotherapy. Again Jesus was carrying me! My stylist was a blessing in my life!

The lessons of humility and surrender that one learns when paralyzed are overwhelming. Did I mention trimming toenails—an otherwise routine task done occasionally as needed without much though or concern, right? Wrong! Unfortunately, when you are paralyzed, your toenails continue to grow. Since your feet are constantly covered by socks in the cold winter months, you never notice that your toenails are getting longer, much longer. Suddenly they are catching on socks, and they begin to hurt. We had to devise a plan for my daughter to trim my toenails.

Similar to a salon, we sat me, with the help of the Hoyer lift, on the couch and soaked my foot in a tub of warm, soapy water. So far, so good. Then my daughter lifted my leg onto the ottoman and prepared to trim my toenails. She was shocked by my screams of terror!

For some reason, I felt so vulnerable because I was unable to move that I imagined her cutting my skin instead of the nails. She became terrified that she was going to hurt me! I had complete feeling in my feet, just no muscle strength to move them. So if she cut me, I could not move my foot out of the way. Somehow we got through it. This became a terrifying and difficult ordeal that we all shudder to remember. But again, just one more thing we take for granted.

The burden of caring for an invalid was overwhelming at times for my family. My heart broke as I watched them struggle to administer medication, fill prescriptions, move me from bed to chair and then chair to bed, make doctor appointments, deal with therapists and nurses coming into the home throughout the week, help me practice my exercises, handle emergencies in the home with electricity and heat, prepare meals, do dishes, shop, do laundry, clean house, greet my friends, keep me entertained, serve my meals, keep my spirits up—all while my husband and son worked full time and my married daughter attended college online full time and lived in my home. We decided to hire an aide to come into the home three times per week for two hours just to prepare and serve breakfast, clean the kitchen, and tend to my needs. We had several different people from a nursing service, but one in particular became part of the family. She provided much needed relief for my girls. She was kind and thoughtful and actually cared about us. It broke our hearts when we had to discontinue her services because the out-of-pocket cost was astronomical. But God sent her to us when we needed her most.

When I became discouraged, my family was there to support me. One day, I cried most of the afternoon and simply couldn't stop. Make no mistake that the grief and loss is something you must get through, and it is not easy or fast. My girls understood and just consoled me that "this too will pass." My son came into the room and said, "Mom, Jesus cried too in the garden of Gethsemane. He asked God to take the cup from Him. And on the cross, He said, 'Father why have you forsaken me?'" I was so encouraged and stunned by my son's insight and recollection of the Bible. God told me that my illness was affecting many people in astounding ways that I could not even see. My children were consoling me with stories from the Bible and scriptures. This was a dream come true for me.

So many of my friends were anxious to visit that we started setting up lunch visits while my daughters were both there to help. Friends from out of town or those nearby would come over for lunch, and we would sit at the dining room table, where my daughters served lunch. This was a pleasant way to converse and comfortable for me to sit at the table in my wheelchair, while they also sat at the table. I began to feel almost normal. This was essential to my mental and emotional healing. I was very grateful and encouraged by these visits. Although I still had much work to do, I was beginning to see that I might actually be walking soon again!

CHAPTER 8

First Steps at Last

Your word is a lamp to my feet, a light to my path.
—Psalm 119:105

Since my return home in November 2014, after four months in the hospital and nursing homes, I had only been out of the house three times to attend doctor appointments. It was already April, and spring was in the air, but it was hard for me to know that since I still was not able to ride in a regular vehicle. The times I went to the doctor, I had to be transported in a special vehicle equipped to accommodate a wheelchair, at seventy-five-dollars-per-trip out-of-pocket. However, that all was about to change.

My physical therapist was working toward a treatment plan during the long months of November through April, which would gradually lead to my mobility. He was a strong Christian, and he never lost faith that I would be able to achieve these goals. (There is that word again—*faith*.) By April, I was doing knee bends at the kitchen sink, and learning to push my wheelchair to the bathroom and use my walker to go into the bathroom on our first floor. He built a small wooden step that I practiced on. Freedom! These small improvements were exhilarating.

Once I could walk with a walker, I practiced relentlessly. My home is a circular pattern in that you can walk from foyer to kitchen to dining room to living room, back to foyer. I went round and round without ceasing. Well, at first, let's say I went one time around and sat down for a rest. The strength that it takes to move the human body in a coordinated fashion is very extensive, and it was long in coming. Everything we take for granted was an effort. Sitting in a chair? For a little while. Standing up? Only with something to hold onto and a big effort. Walking? Only with a walker and baby steps—and only a few before I got winded. It took repetitive practice in this circular pattern to build my strength. But at least I could do it on my own. After a while, my family trusted me enough to let me go without walking behind me.

I learned from Sue how to go out to my front porch. This involved moving my wheelchair to the front door, having someone prop the door open, placing my walker down on the porch (one step down), then putting my feet down onto the porch and standing holding onto the walker. Yikes! I could then take two steps onto the porch and sit in a chair (see picture). These movements would prove essential in the process of learning to go out to the van.

As I prayed each morning and throughout the day, God was encouraging me with verses to move me forward. Hebrews 12: 1–2 tells us, *"Run with perseverance the race marked for us."* Again God was telling me to *run!* God's healing love was pouring over me during this period word.

Verses of faith showered down on me, strengthening and lifting me up:

- *"Fix our eyes not on what is seen, but on what is unseen."* (2 Corinthians 4:18)
- *"Faith is being sure of what we hope for, certain of what we do not see."* (Hebrews 11:1)

- *"Keep your eyes on Jesus."* (Hebrews 12:2)
- *"I am with you always, even unto the end of the age."* (Matthew 28:20)
- *"His sheep will hear his voice."* (John 10:27)
- *"Truly I tell you, if you have faith as small as a mustard seed... nothing will be impossible for you."* (Matthew 17:20)
- *"The Lord will guide you always; he will satisfy your needs in a sun-scorched land and will strengthen your frame. You will be like a well-watered garden, like a spring whose waters never fail."* (Isaiah 58:11)
- *"When my life was ebbing away, you remembered me."* (Jonah 2:7)
- *"Be joyful in hope, patient in affliction, faithful in prayer."* (Romans 12:12)
- *"The faithful prayer of a righteous man avails much."* (James 5:16)

My faith and my hope were growing even as my muscles were strengthening. God was drawing me closer the whole time. He wants us to depend on Him: *"Lean not on your own understanding."* We've been given the gift of *faith*. We know GOD is working on our behalf, just as my therapists were working on my behalf. Faith is the *assurance* of things hoped for—being sure. Faith is like the steel structure that holds up huge high-rises. When you are inside the building, you don't see the steel structure, but it is holding up the building and you depend on it to keep the building standing.

This kind of *faith* and *trust* is supernatural. It is a result of the indwelling Spirit of God living inside each of us. When things seem all wrong, God says, "Trust me anyway!" Trust enables you to live above your circumstances. God is much more interested in a relationship with us than circumstances. God is bigger than our circumstances. *"In this world you will have trouble, but take heart! I have overcome the world"* (John 16:33).

Each month, I was evaluated by the supervisor of the physical therapy team as well as the supervisor of the occupational therapy team. My continued therapy depended on their assessment of my progress, and my ability to benefit from continued therapy. So I was on the fence—I did everything they asked to the best of my ability to demonstrate progress, but I didn't want to lose the therapy sessions, either. I learned that my home therapy would be ending at the end of April. Panic! I was not yet walking well with a walker. How would I get to the next level?

Steve decided I was ready to try something very daring —standing alone. Yikes! He was really pushing me. But I guess because he believed I could do it, I believed I could do it also! So when he arrived each morning, the first thing I had to do before I became exhausted was to stand up from the bed or the wheelchair using the walker, then let go. This was exhilarating and terrifying at the same time. At first when I let go, I felt wobbly and weak and had to grab right back on to the walker. But after a few tries, I could stand alone for ten seconds. Then twenty seconds. Then forty seconds. Each time Steve would start a session with me, he would test me. I finally achieved the goal of standing alone without the walker for two full minutes! I was ecstatic but had to rest for ten minutes to regain my strength. It was worth it!

Steve was very focused on preparing me to ride like a regular passenger in our van. I had not done this in a year. Much discussion went into this step. Was I ready? I knew I could step down to the front porch. Steve worried that I would be too exhausted walking the short distance from the porch to the van, approximately thirty steps with the walker. So he insisted that I use the wheelchair to get to the van, then stand with the walker, then get into the van following his instructions. We had to try! We all knew Steve's precious time with us was coming to an end. I was able to use the walker to step off the porch, then ride in the wheelchair to the van, use the walker to stand again.

So on April 22, 2015, over nine months since the day of my collapse, I was able to get back into the family van. I learned to place a plastic bag on the seat to enable swiveling, then sit down on the seat, and manually lift my legs into the van. I use this procedure to this day (but without the bag). Praise God! I had reached a huge step in my mobility journey. Another awesome milestone!

CHAPTER 9

Fresh Air

Arise! Shine! For your light has come; the glory
of the Lord has dawned upon you.
—Isaiah 60:1

Once I could get into the van and my home therapy ended in May, 2015, I began attending outpatient physical-therapy sessions at the hospital where my life was saved. I received two sessions per week for a period of ten weeks, comprising the twenty sessions allowed by insurance. I also received twenty sessions of occupational therapy to strengthen my arms and my balance. This therapy was much more strenuous, because that is what my body needed at the time. I remember being able to walk around the track using my walker just one time at my first session and having to sit down because my heart was pounding out of my chest. They had to take readings to ensure it was not too stressful for my heart, which was unaccustomed to supporting my body. I never knew how long it would take for my whole body to catch up. It's so much more than just your leg or arm muscles that needs to gain strength—it is your heart as well!

The therapy room at the outpatient physical therapy clinic had a variety of machines and a short flight of steps for practice. I remember looking at the steps on the first day, when I was brought in a wheelchair because it was too far to walk with a walker. I used my wheelchair for several weeks before gaining strength and courage to walk all the way in from the parking lot with a walker. When I first saw those steps, I thought, "If I can just learn to master those steps, it will be a *miracle.*" Not only did I master the steps, I did so by July 4—my goal—so I could walk up the stairs in my home. You see, my bedroom and bathroom were on the *second floor.* I had not been able to go to my room *or* take a shower in *one* year! Needless to say, I could not wait to do so! The steps were a major goal, and with God's help, I eventually achieved it! Another milestone!

Even though I had a long way to go to normal, I knew I had also come a very long way, and I was filled with joy and gratitude to God who was my strong tower through all my days. I knew the healing was coming, even though it was a process, a journey. When I wondered why it took so long, God taught me about patience. He gave me the story of Lazarus, his good friend, who had become ill. Lazarus's two sisters, Mary and Martha, sent for Jesus, saying, *"Jesus, come, the one you love is sick"* (John 12). He loved Lazarus, *yet when he heard this, he stayed where he was for two more days!*

Is this what you would have done if you heard your friend was dying? No, you would have gone immediately. But Jesus waited, and He had a purpose in waiting. When He arrived in Bethany, Lazarus had died and was in the tomb for four days. Mary said, "Lord, if you had been here, my brother would not have died." Jesus was deeply moved when He saw her weeping. Jesus then had them move the stone from the tomb and said, "Lazarus come out!" Jesus did this so the people standing there would know that God had sent Him.

As I struggled to understand the journey of my healing, the Lazarus story filled me with hope and revelation. We do not understand God's ways. Could it be there was a purpose for this very slow recovery? Could it be that He would use my journey for good? Could it be that by the story of my journey of healing, God's power might be revealed and the truth of God's words might become evident? Could it be that others would find encouragement and hope in my words? God's word tells us,

> *For my thoughts are not your thoughts, neither are your ways my ways, declares the Lord. As the heavens are higher than the earth, so are my ways higher than your ways, and my thoughts higher than your thoughts… my word will not return to me empty, but will accomplish what I desire and achieve the purpose for which I sent it.* (Isaiah 55:8–11)

God was reassuring me and telling me that He had a plan for my illness and for my gradual recovery. He loved his friend Lazarus, and He waited. He loved me even more. I could learn to be patient and to wait on his timing.

It took most of the summer for my heart to become strong enough for me to walk without panting. By this time, my life was coming closer to the normal I had known. I slept in my own bed and took my own shower every day, where I could wash my own hair! Four long months of therapy after I had regained muscle strength prepared me to walk without a walker or cane in September 2015. At long last, after one full year, I was walking again! God had healed me! *"Strengthen your feeble arms and weak knees—make level paths for your feet—so the lame will not be disabled, but rather healed"*(Heb. 12:12). God's promises are true!

Throughout my recovery period, I marked my progress by milestones. I didn't always achieve the milestone in the time that I had set, but at least it gave me some type of gauge to chart my journey. For instance, my first goal was to be home and have all my friends over to my house at Thanksgiving 2014 for a dinner that I would prepare to say thanks for praying. Haha! That tells you how far off base I was in my expectations for recovery. Then I thought, "Perhaps I can be walking with a walker by Christmas!" Hah! I overshot that one by about five months! Perhaps these expectations set me up for disappointment, but I never gave up hope! I believe Jesus carried me through these.

After a time, I began to be more reasonable. I wanted to sit in a regular wheelchair instead of the monstrous reclining wheelchair—accomplished! I wanted to be able to put on my jacket myself—accomplished! I wanted to sign my name with a pen—accomplished! I wanted to sit at the kitchen table in the wheelchair—accomplished! I wanted to be able to transfer myself from the bed into the wheelchair and eliminate the Hoyer lift—accomplished! We called the medical supply company to come pick up that Hoyer lift that very day. After I could sit in a regular wheelchair and pull myself up to the sink, I felt that maybe I could walk with a walker by Easter. I was about three weeks shy of meeting that goal on time. Once we knew that I was losing home therapy at the end of April, we all started focusing harder on results. I was walking across the room with a walker by the end of April and able to get into a van with help in May.

Other goals included going to outpatient physical therapy at a facility starting in May; walking up the stairs of my home by July 4, 2015; attending my cousin's anniversary party in Chicago on August 1, 2015; driving by fall; renewing my driver license by November 2015 (so I didn't have to retake the driving test); and going to Atlanta for a fundraiser with my two dear friends in October 2015. By the grace and power of the Almighty God, I met all of these goals. My recovery was truly a work in progress, and the Lord wasn't quite finished with me yet.

CHAPTER 10

Family Reunited

Be joyful in hope, patient in affliction, faithful in prayer.
—Romans 12:12

Don't you just love the way God works? As I mentioned earlier, it seems He is weaving this tapestry that we call our lives. One side rough and unfinished, but the other side a beautiful pattern. Just as with weaving, sewing, painting, baking, or other creative arts, the finished product usually does not appear instantly. It takes time and effort and love on the part of the creator, and so it is with the tapestry of our lives.

Since I heard my first child's cry in 1979, my children have been the center of my life. My husband, my family, my work, and church all took my time and attention, but my children were the main focus, the reason for it all. I thoroughly enjoyed and was fulfilled in my role as mom. Our family was blessed with three healthy children, two girls and one boy.

My oldest daughter was a typical firstborn—intelligent, driven, competitive, and close to us as parents. After all, we spent two years together before her younger sister was born. Jen and I clicked from the time she joined our family and was a very "good" baby (as if any babies are bad). I was very proud of her and counted on her help and ability to be a role model as the oldest child in the family.

Jen excelled at school. Her sixth grade teacher told me at a conference, "What can I say about Jen? She is the perfect student." Beginning in first grade, Jen enjoyed taking part in school musicals, participating in Girl Scouts, playing volleyball, and spending time with friends. In eighth grade, she was invited to participate in an Engineering Day for junior high students at our local university, where her group won first prize with their group project.

When she attended Catholic high school, Jen did well and was on the debate team. After graduating, she was invited back to help judge debates. Jen always had a heart for God and joined our Catholic church on her own following high school graduation. She attended a university about twenty miles from our home, so she commuted back and forth every day to save the cost of room and board. Jen assumed responsibility for all her college expenses and worked part time to avoid taking out any student loans. She was working very hard to make this happen, and I know she felt overwhelmed at times. She established her own savings and checking accounts and handled all financial dealings of any kind on her own without a bit of help from us. She had a great head on her shoulders and was destined for success in whatever she chose.

In high school, Jen dated a little and hung around with friends. At the beginning of her senior year, she met a young man at her place of employment, and they started dating. He lived a little farther out of town, so they saw each other on weekends. He was two years older and was not attending college, and I remember being concerned about what he planned for the future and where the relationship was going. However, I felt very strongly that Jen was approaching adulthood and had to make her own decisions. She was extremely responsible and had a strong heart for God.

When Jen was twenty and finishing her sophomore year in college, she was still dating this young man. It was the year 2000, and on Memorial Day weekend, she had been gone overnight but called me the next day and said, "Mom, I've been staying with some friends, and I'd like you to come see the place." Of course, I hopped in the car and went to meet her.

She greeted me in a small, neat ranch house and showed me around. It was very clean and organized. We went to get coffee, and Jen told me that she was going to be moving in with these friends, and her boyfriend would be one of them. I was very shocked, and we discussed whether this would be the best option for her. Her mind was made up, and she came home to get her things and then moved.

I believe that God wires us mothers with supernatural alarm bells that sometimes go off and ring so loudly that we cannot shut them off! I knew my daughter was a young adult, college age, totally responsible, perfectly equipped to make her own decisions, but I was extremely uncomfortable with what was happening. In my heart, I felt this young man was not a good influence and had convinced her to move to this house. I felt like I was stuck in a bad dream, but I couldn't get out of it. I asked Jen to come home, to reconsider, but she felt this was something she wanted to pursue. There was something very, very wrong.

Over that summer, we saw Jen less and less. She was busy taking a college class, and she was working at the restaurant where all of these friends worked. At the end of the summer, she let me know that she decided to put school on the back burner to pursue her opportunities working with her friends, to see what it held for her. Her boyfriend decided to leave the group later in the summer, but Jen decided to stay.

Throughout this time, my heart was struggling with the intuitive spiritual feeling that this was not God's plan for Jen's life. It was hard for me as a mom, and many of you can identify with these feelings. I was often close to tears, as I was yearning for Jen to leave the group and return to her old life. My head and my heart were telling me that something was not right, and I prayed harder and more insistently than I ever had in my life.

I couldn't figure out what God was doing. It was not like her to make a decision like this. Why couldn't she understand what I was saying? It was like there was a wall, something keeping us apart. My husband and I even went to the house one day and spoke with other members of the group. It came to a heated argument with lots of tears, and we left without Jen. It seemed her friends had much more influence than we did, and it frightened us.

There is a danger that lurks in the world, and though I don't speak of it much in this book, we call it by different names—the devil, Satan, the evil one, the father of lies, the author of confusion, an evil force. As Christians, we know that Satan exists. *"Be alert and of sober mind. Your enemy the devil prowls around like a roaring lion looking for someone to devour"* (1 Pet. 5:8). In my spirit, I clearly knew that this living situation and these choices that Jen was making were not of God, they were the result of evil forces at work. I felt it in my heart and in my soul. The prowling lion had hooked his awful teeth in my daughter, and he was not letting go. Make no mistake, evil forces are very real and are all around us!

Sometimes this prowling lion takes the form of an *insidious force* that draws people away from God. Satan's victory is to draw people away from the one, true God, Jesus Christ. We see it in our world every day—whether it is work, money, success, fame, material goods, beauty, youth, sex, technology, music, alcohol, gambling. *"Any high thing that exalts itself (makes itself more important) than God"* (2 Cor. 10:5). If these things become more important than your walk with God, if they push God out of the no. 1 spot, they become an idol. However, most people do not recognize it. It gradually becomes a strong influence too hard to ignore. People become addicted to whatever brings them pleasure. *"For where your treasure is, there will your heart be also"* (Matt. 6:21). And their hearts turn away from God, without even realizing it.

Sometimes the insidious force can be influential people, telling us what we want to hear. We don't really understand what is happening to us. Jen would tell me years later that there is an insidious force pulling people away from God and she had experienced it. For those who are at a vulnerable stage in their lives, as my daughter Jen was, the strong influence that other people provided changed the trajectory of her life. Jen was young and dealing with confusing feelings for a troubled boyfriend who did not return the same loving feelings. In her effort to help him, she was drawn into a web of influence that was not of God and would end up drawing her away from God for a time. This can be very dangerous by virtue of the fact that it is insidious and appears to be normal. I knew in my heart what was happening, and that it was straight from the evil one, but I was *powerless* to stop it! As a mom who was desperate to save her daughter, I was heartbroken, despondent, and frantic!

One day, I told God that if He wanted me to get through that day, He would just have to give me the strength. I just could not even will my body to get out of bed. I opened my Bible, and one of the first passages I read was, *"My grace is sufficient for you, my power is made perfect in your weakness"* (2 Cor. 12:9).

"What were you saying, Lord?" I wanted Him to tell me He would change her mind, He will get her out of the group, He will bring her home! Instead, He said, "His grace is sufficient," what did that mean? Was I not to ask for my intentions?

After much prayer, and much intercession from friends, I understood that Jesus was telling me that He is all I need. To put anything else at the same level of importance as God—even if it was my precious Jen—was idolatry! I had to learn to release Jen to God's loving arms. Of course, He knew and expected me to pray endless mom prayers—that is the righteous thing to do. But to stop living my life because I could not wade through the grief I felt was wrong. "His grace was *sufficient*." He was all I needed.

He also said, "My power is made perfect in your weakness." So in other words, when I felt the weakest, as I did that summer, God's power would be strongest in me, to keep me going, to survive. I didn't have to think I would be the one to bring Jen home—God would take care of that. His power is *strongest* when we are weak. Jen's leaving was so sudden, so drastic, and the choice was so frightening that it plunged me into depression. But by the power of Jesus Christ, who is ever faithful, who does not lie, and whose words are always true, I survived that summer—and years and years after. God was working the *whole* time. God was in *control* the whole time! But that was a lesson I had yet to learn.

Jen and I continued to see and talk with each other after that summer, and we did continue to try to convince her to leave, with no success. Fortunately, God was helping us to forge a different kind of relationship, founded on unconditional love, such as the way the Father loves us. Jen was always pleasant, and our conversations were positive. We didn't see her as much as we would have liked, but we learned to accept that. We were grateful to see her at all. Our biggest goal was to show Jen in every way that we loved her and would never ever stop loving our precious girl. Nothing she could do would turn our love away!

During all of this time, our heartfelt prayers never ceased. We prayed continuously and fervently. But God was calling me to surrender my precious daughter to Him. Just as He had called Abraham to be willing to sacrifice Isaac, I had to be willing to give up my daughter to Him. She didn't belong to me; she was God's child. I was learning to trust in a way that I could never imagine. It was not easy to give her to God, but we knew we had to. We knew that God has plans for all of us, and we prayed that God's plans for Jen's life would bring us closer together.

We saw Jen on birthday celebrations, Christmas, Easter, and sometimes just for a visit to our house. We talked occasionally on the phone, but Jen was very busy. We didn't discuss anything too personal and kept most conversations superficial but pleasant. When my son graduated from high school in 2008, Jen came to the graduation party at our house. Everything went well, and she told us that she and the other friends would be moving to Tennessee soon, as they had a business opportunity there. By this time, I had prayed to the point that I was able to truly surrender my daughter to my Lord, Jesus Christ. Although she would be farther away in miles, she was ever so close in my heart. With promises to come and say good-bye before they left, Jen went back to the house. They left for Tennessee a few weeks later, in the summer of 2008.

Since we were all working full time, we could only visit each other a couple of times per year. We visited Jen in Tennessee and toured the Smokey Mountains, Gatlinburg, and Pigeon Forge. We all enjoyed our time together. Jen invited us to their home in Tennessee and cooked a delicious meal for us. She visited our home in Ohio over the Christmas holidays.

In 2012, twelve years after Jen left our home, she sent me an e-mail saying that she was moving out of the home with her friends and into an apartment with a roommate. She also told me about a man she had known for several months who was a strong family man, a Christian, and they were enjoying a nice relationship as they got to know each other. My heart melted. I felt the sword of the Almighty God was wielding results. God was shining his laser light of truth into her life. Jen's heart was being touched by God, and her life would be changing. I was ecstatic! God had been working all along.

Another e-mail several months later told more about this wonderful man and how deeply they cared for each other. He had proposed. She sent pictures of the ring. We would meet him that Christmas, and they would marry the following April. God had answered my prayers from long ago in ways I could never have imagined. Not only was Jen an active part of our family again, she told us of how strong and powerful her relationship was with Jesus. Her experiences had brought her even closer to Him. *"Now glory be to God who by this mighty power at work within us s able to do far more than we would ever dare ask or even dream of—infinitely beyond our highest prayers, desires, thoughts, or hopes"* (Eph. 3:20). The marriage of Jen and Alan was attended by my entire family, and it was a celebration of God's love and power. But that was only the beginning!

When I first became ill in July 2014, Jen was living with her husband in Tennessee, attending college. She came to visit and help out that fall. But after Christmas, when I was at home, it was apparent that my family needed her help. Jen worked out with her professors to take her classes online (even though they were not online classes), and she came to Ohio to stay at my home for six months to care for me. This girl whom I had beseeched God to save ended up becoming my caregiver in the darkest, most difficult time of my life. She selflessly took care of my every need for six months. We talked, and Jen said if she had still been living with her friends at the time of my illness, she probably would not have been able to take six months to care for me. God's plan and His timing are *perfect.* Don't ever doubt that He has every detail of our lives under control.

Now that I am healed, we enjoy a vibrant and fulfilling relationship with Jen and Alan and visit back and forth often. We are waiting to see what God has in store for the future of our family. People often tell me that I am a walking miracle—that I was near death, paralyzed for a year, and now I am well. But I don't know in my heart which is the greater miracle—that God healed me or that He brought Jen back to us and to a deep relationship with her Creator? I am grateful to God because His mercies are new every day!

The other members of my family were reunited as well in a deeper, more profound way. While I was in a coma for a month, my husband became the rock of our family. He kept watch at the hospital day and night, keeping friends and family informed through constant text blasts. He would end every text with a spiritual thought, "If God is for me, who can be against? Hands up, knees down!" People marveled at his strength and his faith. He then stood by me daily throughout my recovery period.

My younger daughter battles bipolar depression, and even though this was terribly stressful for her as well as everyone else, she never left my side. She was my constant companion after I went home and often sat with me as I cried to encourage me with positive thoughts. She shared coping strategies with me, and they helped. I benefitted from having my own personal counselor.

In addition, my two daughters had six months in which to live together and share the duties of caring for Mom. This was not easy! But during that time, they came to know and understand each other much better. God was weaving that tapestry again.

My son was at my side as well once I returned home, but he worked full time and had to visit in the evenings. He always told me I would get better if I just took the medicine the way the doctor told me to. He also told me about dreams he had about me and how he saw me walking across the living room. He came over that day and asked if I had walked. I said no. He said the dream was so real he knew it would happen. Within four weeks, I was walking with a walker.

The toll that profound illness can take on a family can be devastating and should not be minimized. But God is always there if we seek Him, even in the darkest night. God blessed our family in remarkable ways and guided us to work together with calm heads to figure out each problem and support each other when needed. One of the biggest blessings from my illness is the closeness of my family. God's tapestry is turning out to be beautiful.

CHAPTER 11

Summer of Recovery

You keep track of all my sorrows. You have collected all my tears
in your bottle. You have recorded each one in your book.
—Psalm 56:8

It was a summer storm, the kind that pops up from nowhere and disappears just as quickly. As the rain fell on the roof during the summer cloudburst, my eyes went to the plant outside my front door. My younger daughter helped me plant that little red plant one month earlier, and it was not an easy task. Something so routine for most was a huge accomplishment for me. I sat in my wheelchair and she helped me lower the plants into the large pot. I was so grateful to be able to do something useful, something approximating normal. I was proud of that plant. It brought me great joy!

As I observed the delicate red flowers succumbing to the torrent of water gushing from the overflowing gutter, my heart was heavy. Those little flowers would never survive the beating of pounding rain! They were drooping, and several had fallen off the stems. I said a simple prayer asking that Jesus would save that plant that I had planted with great difficulty just a few weeks earlier. Sitting in the wheelchair in my foyer looking out the glass door, I marveled at the rain dancing off the pavement, the scent and the sound of the downpour. I marveled at the majesty of God's creation. But I still worried about my plant! Would it die?

I also reflected on the fact that I now had the time to ponder such things! Before my illness, my life had been so hectic with a demanding full time job and family priorities always doing battle for my time. I would never give a thought to how the rain affected a plant or even if it was raining. The days became a blur of work, meetings, dinners, laundry, etc., etc. Without wanting it to be so, life was passing by without a moment to notice the truly beautiful, simple, important things. Now I had time to observe a summer shower and hear the soothing sound of the rain on the windows. The Lord told me in His Word, *"I will give you hidden treasures, riches stored in secret places, so that you may know that I am the Lord, the God of Israel, who summons you by name"* (Isa. 45:3). He was teaching me, and I was listening, because I had time to listen. He made it clear that He speaks all the time, but I did not always listen.

Two hours later, the rain had long stopped and the sun returned. After we had finished dinner, and I was able to load the dishes into the dishwasher, I went to check on the little red flowers and my plant. A miracle! The sun had warmed the plant, and the flowers again stood at attention. Jesus answered my very simple request, but I realized that in doing so, He was teaching me a lesson. The story of the plant became a metaphor for my life.

Just like my plant, my life had been going well. I was healthy and happy. At least I *believed* I was in control of my everyday life. For the plant, the sun was good, the flowers grew tall and strong and were full of color. All of a sudden, the cloudburst of rain came. The rain came fast and hard, and the water was so heavy the flowers could not remain standing. They just fell over in the water, and some of them perished. My life was going well until all of a sudden, I collapsed with a catastrophic illness! I also could not withstand the heavy illness, and

I fell over. My body almost did not survive. All body systems shut down, and I was on life support. Some aspects of my life were lost.

For the plant, the sun's rays and warmth were all it needed to be revived. We serve a creator who cares about all the details of His creation! *"Look at the birds of the air, they do not sow or reap to store away in barns, and yet your heavenly Father feeds them. Are you not much more valuable than they?"* (Matt. 6:26). The plant continued to live according to God's plan.

After I collapsed, my journey to being "revived" was much more complicated, long, and difficult. But humans are more complex creatures than plants, although we serve the same Creator! God's love and faithfulness did not fail me, and I was being healed throughout the process of my recovery. I am certain that the lessons and insights gained throughout the process brought me to a place of intimacy and knowledge of my Savior that would have been impossible to achieve any other way.

Other things that I had not done for years became the focus of my day. I was still weak at the beginning of the summer, and the out-patient therapy often wore me out. But I was able to do some baking, and I began making my husband's lunches every day. He came to enjoy this treat so much that I still do it to this day. Not only does it save money in the food budget, as opposed to buying lunch, it also helps to ensure that we are eating good, healthy foods. A different kind of life seemed to be unfolding for me.

Physically, I was making steady, encouraging improvements. I had blood drawn in my home every six weeks and saw my doctors every three months. They were keeping a close watch on me and "my numbers." Praise God for competent, attentive doctors. My medications had stabilized, and I was not having any side effects. Even though I took fifteen pills in the morning and six at dinner, they didn't bother me, and it was a small price to pay to avoid a relapse. My doctor said my illness was so bad and chance of relapse was so high that he would keep me on the maintenance-medication regimen for the rest of my life (see appendix B). I learned to accept that. My hair had grown back, and I was gaining strength every day, and I was profoundly grateful.

Mentally and emotionally, I was struggling. While I was immensely grateful and in awe of Almighty God, who had preserved my life and was healing me day by day, I didn't understand what had happened to me or why. And I didn't know what my future held. Looking back, I would learn that what motivated me to speed up the recovery process was the hope that I would return to my job at the child care company. That job was my identity in more ways than I even understood.

In May 2015, I invited the owner of the child care company where I worked to join me for lunch at my home. Jen had gone back home to Tennessee, so this one was all on me. I spent the morning preparing croissant sandwiches, salad, side dishes, and dessert. I set the dining room table and lit candles. Although I was still in a wheelchair, I was determined to walk to the door with my walker just to show her that I could. We ate a nice lunch and enjoyed the food, conversation, and ambiance. When we spoke of the company, I told her that I missed it and that I needed to work. She spoke of closed doors, and God's will. I got the distinct feeling that there was no future for me there.

I was heartbroken! I love the company, the mission, and the people. It had been my life for so long that it was a part of my identity as a person. What was God doing in my life? I was grateful for surviving the coma, grateful for physical recovery, grateful for emotional support of family and friends, but where was my life going now? If I didn't have a job, what would I do? We needed income, and I needed a purpose. This began the third phase of my long recovery.

Emotional and mental recovery is the last and longest portion of coming back from a catastrophic illness such as I experienced. I heard a man speak once who had lost his legs and wore prosthetic legs. He said his physical injuries and adapting to the new legs took about two years, but the emotional trauma he experienced took five years to heal When the illness lingers, the goal is just to return to normal. When normal no longer exists, you must embrace a new normal. God had proven to me over and over again that He was faithful and He was in control. Would I believe Him even for this? When my old boss drove away from my house that day, I could hear God whisper, "Do you still trust me?"

A package was dropped off on my front porch mid-summer, and it contained a memory book that had been created at the corporate office where I worked. It contained some fun pictures of my coworkers and lovely quotes from each of them about their memories of me. It was a beautiful and touching book. I have read it many times, and I treasure it. But at that time, it cemented the fact that I was no longer a part of the organization. Truly, it was a fond farewell. Although I treasure the sentiment and the words of my dear coworkers, my heart broke in two.

Throughout the summer, I prayed for God's leading in my life. One Sunday in church, I wept softly throughout the worship songs as well as throughout the message. I felt so lost, like a boat without an anchor, adrift at sea. A sweet woman sitting behind me passed me a note that said, "I am here for you. I'm praying for you. Let's talk after the service." Debbie and I talked for a long time. She led me to the pastor, who prayed over me as well. They assured me that God would reveal his will for my life in his time—that I shouldn't rush it. At this time, I was still walking with a walker, so I am sure they thought I was very distraught—and I was! Every day I would pray and ask that I would know what He wanted me to do with my life.

A woman who had worked with me at the same child care company about ten years prior to this had started a ministry for women. She was a very strong Christian, a kind and godly woman, and good friend, so I visited her at her outreach center for women. She told me about how God had worked in her life to establish and grow this outreach. She was amazed and thrilled with the miracle of my recovery, as she had visited when I was very ill. Mary convinced me that I should tell my story, that other people would be very encouraged by it. Many other people throughout my illness and recovery had also told me to write my story because my illness was so drastic and my recovery so complete. On my way home from Mary's that day, I thought, "Who will want to read my story? So I got sick and I got better. So what?" God told me very clearly that day in the car, "It's not about you, silly! It's about Me!" I knew I had to write about God's great power and glory in my healing and recovery.

At the beginning of August, my cousin was hosting a fiftieth anniversary party on a touring boat docked at Navy Pier in Chicago. This was a beloved cousin whom I had not seen for quite some time, yet we shared wonderful childhood memories. When I received the "Save the Date" card in March, I could not imagine how I would attend. But I made up my mind that if I could, I would. After sitting in the house for a year, I really wanted to go to Chicago. By the time August 1, 2015, arrived, I had improved enough to ride in the van and to walk with a walker. But could I survive a four-hour trip in the van? How would I be affected? Would I be in pain?

The Chicago trip had been a goal of mine, so my husband drove us to Chicago, and I was able to attend the party on the boat—and what a party! It was magnificent. Although I had to be pushed on the pier in a wheelchair because my legs were too weak to walk, it felt like a celebration of freedom! We were able to stay in a hotel. The trip was great all around, and something that my husband and I needed after our tumultuous year. This was the first time I had travelled since my illness, and it was a milestone in my recovery. I thought about the fact that last August 1, just one year prior, I was just coming out of a coma and unable to move, speak, or breathe. Although the year felt endless as I was going through it, God had carried me through to the next August when I could enjoy a party in Chicago. That is truly miraculous! My extended family couldn't believe I came, but they were blessed by my recovery and told me I looked better than I ever had. Praise God for miracles!

In September, my daughter Jen and her husband, Alan, invited us to visit them over Labor Day weekend. We traveled to Tennessee and had a wonderful time. We stayed in a hotel with a pool, and because I loved swimming, my husband helped me into the pool on several of the days. I felt blessed beyond measure to be able to swim again. Not only could I carefully step into the pool with help, I could sit in the sun without a reaction. Several medications that I take carry the warning that they might cause photosensitivity. I enjoy sitting in the sun, and God has allowed me to continue without any side effects. Thank you, Jesus!

We attended church with Jen and Alan, where I enjoyed hearing Jen sing in the choir. What a blessing! Jen then stood up and introduced me as her mom for whom they had all been praying. They clapped. I told them the verse that had kept me going was this: *"Those who wait upon the Lord shall renew their strength; they shall mount up with wings like eagles; they will run and not be weary; they shall walk and not faint"* (Isa. 40:31). That verse was for me. He told me I will be walking again. I hung onto those words as his promise, and his promises are true!!

God was blessing me, healing me, and teaching me patience and trust. God was so good to me! He was telling me to trust Him and not fear. Throughout that summer, though I was making physical progress, I was in the middle of fierce spiritual battles, and Satan's greatest pleasure was to instill fear and steal my joy. My despair was Satan's victory. I would not let him win. God tells us to *"resist the devil and he will flee from you"* (James 4:7). The Bible also tells us that struggles will produce perseverance. I really struggled, but I knew even in my struggles, I was not alone. I sensed that Jesus was carrying me, and He would not let me down. God is faithful. I needed to resist fear, rebuke the devil, and trust God's plan for my life. I told Satan, "You will not steal my joy—I rebuke you!" I repeated this whenever I felt low in my spirit. So easy to say those words, but to know and experience them in my heart was something I could only do through prayer. You see, *hope* is always stronger than *fear*, and hope in the God of the universe will carry us through anything. Remember, our GOD is *bigger*!

CHAPTER 12

No Room at the Inn

Do not remember the former things, nor consider the things of old. Behold I do a new thing, now it shall spring forth. Shall you not know it? I will even make a road in the wilderness, and rivers in the desert.
—Isaiah 43: 18–19

"There's no place like home, there's no place like home!" is the popular line from the epic production *The Wizard of Oz*. Poor little Dorothy is hurled by a tornado into a strange and foreign land complete with witches, flying monkeys, and a wizard. She is accompanied by the scarecrow, the tin man, and the cowardly lion, her only true friends. They tried to help her navigate all the pitfalls of the Land of Oz, but all Dorothy wanted to do was find her way home. When she finally put on the red shoes and clicked her heels, she could say, "There's no place like home!" and be magically transported back to Kansas.

With my sudden and catastrophic illness, I felt a little like Dorothy in a strange land. I was transported into a world of doctors, hospitals, medications, machines, illness, and paralysis. Believe me, all I wanted to do was go home. Like Dorothy, I was blessed to have dear friends at my side who were pulling me through the confusion, but for me, there was no going back to Kansas. Although I left the hospital and returned to my physical home, my job and career were gone.

My illness and recovery were very long, and the thought of returning to my normal life was a motivating factor in my physical therapy. Even so, it was about a year before I could consider getting around again. When I spoke to my employer at lunch at my home back in May, she was not encouraging about my return. The company had made other plans. There was no room for me. I had been working toward a goal that wasn't there.

Because of the emotional, physical, and financial impact of my sudden illness, my family and I were all devastated. We were unprepared for the drastic turn that our lives had taken. The position I held for so long had become a lifestyle. As I said earlier, I loved the company, the mission, and all of the staff. I derived much pleasure and comfort from being among like-minded individuals, doing important work that affected children and families. I felt blessed to be able to work for a company where the name of Jesus was honored, and I could share my faith. The company owner and I had travelled together and socialized at times. We had worked closely for twenty-six years. She knew about my family, and I knew about hers. She was very supportive when my daughter Jen left and then when my daughter Ali was diagnosed with bipolar depression. It took me a very long time and lots of tears and prayers over that summer and beyond to internalize and accept that this company was no longer part of my life.

God was carrying me through this difficult, emotional grieving period as He had through my physical illness, by reminding me that His word is full of stories of people who had heartbreaking difficulties and survived through God's power. His Word is meant to be God speaking His life into us. The Bible provides a wealth of stories offering insight, direction, and encouragement. Since the Bible is the inerrant word of God, it is as if God is telling us these stories Himself to teach us and console us when we are lost.

Job is one of the most famous stories and helped me to see my own circumstances from another perspective. Job was the character in the bible who was a wealthy landowner, with many livestock, flocks, grains, buildings, and many children. He was considered by his friends to be fortunate, respected, and very blessed by God. In other words, he had a great life and was happy. Job was a faithful servant to God, yet Satan told God that if Job lost everything, he would curse God. God told Satan, *"There is no one on earth like him, he is blameless, a man who fears God and shuns evil"* (Job 1:8).

God allowed Satan to test Job but said he must spare his life. Satan caused Job to lose his flock and all his children to die. Job lost everything. He then caused Job to become ill with boils all over his body. Job's own wife said, *"Curse God and die!"* (Job 2:9). Yet Job responded, *"Shall we accept good from God and not trouble?"* (Job 2:10). Even Job's three good friends came to him and said he must have done something wrong for God to be so mad at him. It is important to note that at one point, Job looks back with fondness on a better time in his life. He remembers the good old days when he was prosperous and respected and spent lots of time with his very close family.

Can I tell you how often I had the same thoughts? When you are suffering, it is easy to remember the good old days, as Job did. In my case, the feelings of rejection were overwhelming. I lost sense of who I was. The memories of the past can keep us chained to despair and longing. I couldn't understand why I was losing that vital part of my life. The grief and loss took quite a toll on me, yet I continued to seek God's comfort and peace. My friends helped a great deal. God gives us a memory—it is a gift to remember wonderful things! I had many such memories of my former career, the people I worked with, the financial freedom that came with my income—but when we get stuck on remembering what used to be, it can prevent us from being open to the blessings of today and the promises of tomorrow. God is not finished with us yet! He has plans for each one of us.

Job finally thanked God for his life situation and praised Him. Job replied, *"He knows the way that I take, and when He has tested me, I shall come forth as gold"* (Job 23:10). Because of Job's faithfulness throughout all his trials, God rewarded him. He gave Job twice as much as he had before. He had many more children and grandchildren. God blessed the latter part of Job's life more than the first part.

So what did Job have to do with me? Although there were similarities in my life, I am far from the "blameless servant" that Job was. I love God with all my heart and have tried to do his will. Yet with my illness, I felt I had lost everything. At one point, I had lost my health, my breathing, my speaking, my moving, my eating or drinking, and now my livelihood. How was I to respond? I, too, had wonderful memories and longed for the past. I felt despair and disappointment. As I pleaded with God over that summer to show me His will, to provide a light to my path, I felt Him calling me to trust and to have *faith*, as Job did. He tells us in Matthew 17:20, *"I tell you the truth, if you had faith even as small as a mustard seed, you could say to this mountain 'Move from here to there,' and it would move. Nothing would be impossible."* Nothing? Nothing would be impossible? Then maybe there was something else for me? Maybe there was a job for me? Jesus, increase my faith!

I thought about Job giving thanks to God and I pondered, how in the world could he be giving thanks after all he went through? The Bible tells us *"In everything give thanks, for this is the will of God in Christ Jesus concerning you"* (1 Thess. 5:18). But if Job didn't give thanks *for everything* that happened, he gave thanks in *everything*. God knows every thought and feeling we have and doesn't want us to feel pain. But sometimes that pain results in a greater good, which we cannot yet see. We trust his plan. Giving thanks in everything demonstrates our trust in His power and His plan for our lives.

God was reminding me again as He had done throughout my life that *his* grace is *sufficient* for me! He is all I need—and He will be everything I need. I leaned on that with all my heart. My dear friends were the lifeline that I needed to survive this turbulent period in my life. When I was working, I prayed every single morning for years for 'strength, energy, wisdom, and courage. God provided all these qualities in the close friends who nurtured my heart in my darkest days. A very close friend had the strength to remind me to stay strong, another had the energy to keep me laughing and busy with lunches and visits, and the other friend had the courage to get me connected into a network of professionals to start networking again. These friends embodied the very attributes that I had prayed for. God answered my prayers. We enjoyed each other's company, prayed for each other, cheered each other on, had lunches and dinners, celebrated birthdays, and more. These people provided the true emotional *life support* that I needed. They are blessings and angels in my life.

My professional passion has always been early childhood education (see appendix C). I studied, read, and trained in the field for so many years that it became deeply embedded in my heart and mind. The company I worked for was a high end, very high quality educational facility, and everyone on our team was a like-minded individual to various degrees. Therefore, when I could not return to my former job, I missed the field of ECE as well. One of my friends was doing work with young children in a nonprofit ministry and brought the director of the program to my home. Though I was still in a wheelchair at the time, I could type on my laptop, and together we decided that I would be able to write grants for the organization. I had never done that kind of writing before, but I was excited about the challenge.

Today I am still writing grants for this organization that serves a very low-income population in the inner city, providing parenting education, child care, preschool, and wrap-around social services. I am thrilled to be part of the group that is making this happen. I believe totally that we will only break the chains of generational poverty through education and stronger families.

I have also had the opportunity to do some grant-writing for another organization that is supporting orphans in Haiti. The founder of this program is a sister of a dear friend and has an amazing God-given love and passion for the plight of these children. She is devoting her life to this worthy cause. She is blessed, and she is a blessing. Because of my deep admiration of the founder and the people who run this organization, I am committed to helping in any way. God is showing me different things and calling me in new ways.

Still I longed to be back in the field of early childhood on a professional basis. Because I wanted to remain in the field of early childhood education, I attended a free two-day training session in Dayton, Ohio, in October of 2015. As soon as I walked in the door and observed the chaos of over a hundred teachers and administrators trying to find the right training rooms and materials, I felt I was home. These were my people! I had worked with teachers and administrators my whole career, and being back among them was exhilarating!

In the hallway I ran into a former colleague and center owner from the Dayton area, who offered to take me to lunch. Before my illness, she and I were both in the same advocacy organization and had worked together numerous times. She asked if I would be interested in a position that was open within the organization for executive director. I said, of course, just send me an email with more information. Then for the next six weeks I heard nothing, so I put it on the back burner.

The day before Thanksgiving, I received a phone call saying that the president of the board of the organization wanted to discuss the position and do a phone interview with me. We talked, and I accepted the position of executive director. I was blessed to be able to work remotely from home and become the first person hired into this position in the history of the organization. I am currently enjoying this work and have the opportunity to speak with child care directors and owners every day. My background and personality has prepared me perfectly for this work. I recently coordinated a legislative visit campaign in which I facilitated state legislators visiting child care providers at their place of business to discuss issues in preparation for state-budget voting the following year. They then submitted pictures of the visits, which were posted on social media. This was a very rewarding and fun experience for me. God had provided me with the perfect position for this season of my life, in the field that I love, and I am grateful!

In addition, some consulting opportunities with other child care centers have arisen to challenge my financial and management expertise and provided the interesting work and financial reward I need. God comes to us through the people and events in our lives if we open our hearts and hands to his leading.

God provided the faith of my friends to lift me up, the light to my path for this new opportunity, and the strength, energy, wisdom, and courage to carry on. He is forever faithful and will make a way in the wilderness. He is always in control. He is calling us all the time. Do you hear Him?

CHAPTER 13

Called to be Witnesses

I can do all things through him who strengthens me.
—Philippians 4:13

Why did God save me? Why did He heal me? Throughout my extremely long and slow-moving recovery period, I asked myself this question many times. I was filled with awe and gratitude. I knew that ARDS has up to a 90 percent mortality rate. I knew my condition of vasculitis was extremely rare, and the doctors had been baffled. I knew God's hand was on every medical team member who attended me because they were dedicated and relentless to find the cause and treatment I needed. I knew there were no guarantees I would survive or that I would walk again. I had much to be grateful for. And I praised God every single day for all He had done for me and my family. But I pondered in my heart, why? And even more, why me?

Of course, the Lord, in his infinite grace and mercy, responded to the prayers of hundreds of those who were praying for me. Yes, he spared me for the sake of my husband and children. But I believe God saved me for two reasons: (1) to show his power and glory, (2) because He has more work for me to do on this earth.

First of all, when looking at the Bible, miracles demonstrated to the observers the power and might of God. And not just little things, either—we're talking about parting of the Red Sea, manna from heaven for the Israelites' daily food, the burning bush (that didn't burn), David and Goliath, Daniel in the lion's den (who survived), healing of the lame man in Acts 3, turning water into wine at the wedding feast of Cana, raising Lazarus from the dead, and many more. To the people of Bible times, these were great and mighty displays of God's power, which convinced them that He was real. Life was difficult, they didn't have the communication systems we do today, and many of them could not read. Information was passed as word of mouth, from town to town, even from generation to generation.

We often think that miracles in Bible times were everyday experiences, yet they were not. We forget the fact that the Bible is the recorded history of God's revelation to man, and it happened over centuries. Because we read it in a few chapters, we believe that miracles were happening nonstop. They were not constant, and they were definitely not normal events. So even though we believe the time period depicted in the Bible is full of miracles on a daily basis, they were not quite so frequent. People mostly lived ordinary lives, just as we live ordinary lives.

Miracles happened in the Bible to *prove God's sovereign power and might* and to back up his disciples and prophets, who were His messengers. God is forever trying to draw us into a relationship with Him, and to make His power known to people of Bible times, He had to show His hand. He had to go beyond the "normal" to demonstrate His might. He had to provide proof that what His messengers were saying were right!

Miracles are not normal phenomena, because if they were, they would just be normal. God needed to establish His power in Bible times by demonstrating things beyond normal by performing miracles. God can and does do the same thing today if we are paying attention.

Today, some would say we live among the miraculous—wireless Internet, jets travelling the world, Skype, Facetime, Facebook, Instagram, Twitter, smart boards, remote controls, microwave ovens, smart phones and smart houses, cars driving themselves soon! Imagine the normal of the 1800s in America compared to the normal of today in America!! Normal today would have been called miraculous hundred plus years ago.

Because we do not see dramatic burning bushes or water changing into wine in our everyday lives, we think miracles are no longer happening. Did you know that in many parts of the world, Christians are claiming to see miracles, especially missionaries? When we open our eyes and hearts to the hand of God, we can see miracles happening among us.

In my case, God performed a mighty miracle. How did we know it was a miracle? My healing defied everything that was normal for my drastic and sudden illness. I developed ARDS which normally can be deadly. I couldn't take in oxygen, which normally can lead to brain damage or be deadly. Doctors kept thinking it was pneumonia and bombarding me with antibiotics as I continued to decline, because they didn't know what else to do, which can be deadly. My kidneys failed, my heart went into A-fib, I kept getting worse, which can be deadly. My condition was so bad I was unrecognizable. At the last moment, God delivered a breakthrough in a diagnosis from the Mayo Clinic. Proper treatments were administered, and even though my body had been ravaged by illness, the treatments worked, and I survived. Through all of this, God was demonstrating His mighty power. The prayers that were said by hundreds asking for a miracle were answered!

My illness was sudden and drastic. I was healthy and working. I was eating well and walking every morning. My collapse was dramatic and profound. I was put on life support within twenty-four hours. The doctors couldn't find what was wrong, but my lungs wouldn't take oxygen. I would die if they didn't find resolution. Finally, after much prayer over several weeks, God began to shine the light on the cause of my illness and appropriate treatment.

➢ My lungs began to accept oxygen. *Miraculously, the treatments worked.*

➢ My body had been so damaged by illness, strong drugs, and treatment that they didn't know if I would survive or if I would regain balance and strength in my organs and body systems. *Miraculously, I did.*

➢ They didn't know if my brain and my mind had been permanently damaged from the lack of oxygen, the paralytics, and the illness. Frequently, there is permanent damage. They didn't know if I would regain consciousness or if I would be okay. *Miraculously, I did and I was.*

➢ They didn't know if I would respond with strength and be able to breathe on my own again after being on life support for so long. *Miraculously, I was.*

➢ They didn't know the extent of the damage done to my body by the paralytics, to my muscles (which had atrophied), my spine, my joints. They didn't know for sure if I would fully recover the use of my body. *Miraculously, I did.*

➢ I didn't know if my hair would grow back and if I could take care of myself again. *Miraculously, it did and I am.*

➢ They didn't know if I would walk with balance, with speed, and strength, if I would ever be free of a walker or cane, or if I would drive again. *Miraculously, I did.*

➢ They didn't know if the stress and the trauma would render me useless, a shadow of my former self. They didn't know if I would be able to work again, if I could be productive in my life. *Miraculously, I am.*

- They didn't know if the medications that maintain my health would give side effects, or if I would be able to achieve remission while on this medication. *Miraculously, I did and I am.*

God saved me in every way, and my healing is a miracle. I am a miracle. God is almighty, all-knowing, powerful healer, and I am healed.

That brings me to the second reason God saved me—because He has more work for me to do. Part of that work is to bring praise and glory to His name and to be His witness. God gave me the miracle of healing because He wants me to tell everyone about it! God wants His power and glory to be known to everyone who hears this story because He wants to draw everyone into a relationship with Him! I am called to witness.

Circle back to earlier in my story where I quoted Acts 3. After the lame man has his sight restored, he jumps us and down and tells everyone, and *"All the people were astonished and came running to them"* (Acts 3:11). But Peter says, *"Men of Israel, why does this surprise you?... We are witnesses of this. By faith in the name of Jesus, this man whom you know and see was made strong. It is Jesus name and the faith that comes through him that has given this complete healing to him, as you all can see"* (Acts 3:16). God healed me by His might and power, and He wants me to tell everyone this good news so they also will have faith in God.

There is a saying that when you come through a storm, you may not know how you survived or even if the storm is over yet, but you come out of the storm a different person than when you went in. My illness turned my life upside down in a way nothing else ever has. I lost the ability to navigate my life, and I had to hand that power over to others—to my doctors, to my family, to God. I was no longer in control.

The storm in my life taught me many lessons:

1. *God's grace is sufficient.* When God is all you have, you have all you need! By keeping my eyes on Jesus, I found my way through the storm. I know that He saved me to tell this story!

2. *Sense of the urgency of time.* This was a profound message inherent in the suddenness of my illness. Don't take anything for granted! We do not know that we have tomorrow—or tonight, for that matter. Only God knows the day and hour that we will leave the earth, and it is critical to tell those you love how you feel. It is urgent to forgive those who have hurt you, and ask forgiveness. It is important to have all your affairs in order. Your life today can change *drastically* in a heartbeat!

3. *My husband is my rock.* My husband has been gifted with strength and perseverance. He is logical and strong. He sticks to things no matter what. When he played football in high school, the players would bounce off him as he blocked a play. But throughout my illness and recovery, he was remarkable. I depended completely on him, and he came through. I knew he was caring for me, and I felt safe—I didn't have to worry. He was compassionate, caring, and positive. He made me laugh when I needed it and bore my tears when I needed to cry. I will never forget the way he cared for me in every way. Praise God for my husband!

4. *Family matters.* My children literally cared for me throughout my recovery on a daily basis in every way imaginable. I'm not sure how I would have survived without them, physically, emotionally, or mentally. My daughter who was separated from us for so many years was restored and

took a major role in my recovery. Because of caring for me and spending so much time at the hospital with medical personnel, she has decided to go into nursing and is completing her degree. My younger daughter often counseled me when my spirits were very low. Our family has come to know each other on a much deeper level and are stronger than ever before. God is good! I am honored to have been blessed with children who truly care for me.

5. *Priorities change.* I lost things I thought I could never live without—my job, my income, my hair. But I did *not* lose the most important thing—my God. The most important things in life are not tangible, and they cannot be bought with money. My health is compromised; our financial situation is extremely limited. But my family has each other! We learned to take care of each other in new and different ways. Things that were taken for granted before are now the most important, and things that were so important have fallen off the radar. O. J. Brigance, in his book *Strength of a Champion*, says it well: "Adversity introduces you to yourself." Not only do you learn about yourself, but you learn very quickly what is truly most important. I have God, my family, and my friends. I am happy. I have all I need. God's grace truly is sufficient for me.

6. *Friends show their true colors.* I am blessed to have many friends who care about me and who have prayed for me and supported me in other ways. But my truest friends rallied around me in a way I have never experienced. They showed me strength, energy, wisdom, and courage. They told me to stay strong, they brought me lunches, they helped me financially, they had fundraisers for me, they gave me gifts, they called often, they texted constantly, they told me they loved and missed me. When I could get

into a van, they picked me up and took me places! They were angels sent from heaven. They brought me through this storm—they were God's hands and hearts extended to me in a *real* way. Not everyone who calls themselves a friend rises to the occasion, and that is terribly disappointing. Those I expected to be there were not. But again, I learned a life lesson about the true meaning of friendship.

7. *Comfort zone.* I was happy and comfortable in my job and career, happy with my family, and I thought my life would continue on its path until a ripe old age when I would retire. My career was a large part of my identity, and I thought I could never possibly live any other way. God had other plans (Job had the same situation). And you know what? I was forced out of my comfort zone, and with God's help, I survived. We are stronger than we think we are. I am now networking with other professionals on my own. I no longer represent my company, I represent myself, and I get professional recognition for my own skills and talents. I've learned that I can do other things, and I am good at them! I have leaned on God in ways I never thought possible, and He has always provided what I need. There is a difference between a want and a need. We don't always get what we want, but God provides what we need.

8. *God's mercies are new every morning.* Every day brings a new opportunity to praise God and to experience His love for us. A wise pastor once told me, "God has surprises for you every day." I do not know what the future holds. That much I have learned. But do I trust God with my future? Absolutely! My God who has brought me through so much difficulty, "through many dangers, toils and snares," as the song "Amazing Grace" says. This God who has never let me down is *not* going to let me down now. He has a plan

for my life, and I am going to start by praising his name and giving thanks every day for the miracle of my life. The pastor of my church extolled us to take part in "expectant living"—to keep our hands and hearts open to God for whatever tomorrow brings. Lord Jesus, my hands are open, and I am all yours!

I am convinced that God spared me to give voice to the power of prayer, to the mighty healing power of our God, to teach others about vasculitis, and to give a foundation to the truth of God's promises.

God has carried and spoken to me throughout my illness, healing, and very long and painful recovery. He continues to carry me daily. I am always safe with Him. He reminded me that I am HIS, and I will never forget:

H - *Healing our hearts*

I - *Intimacy and inspiration*

S - *Strength and spirit*

My younger daughter, who was at my bedside daily, providing care and comfort, shared this prayer with me:

"Father God, break me up, O Lord, and pull the fragments close. Let my scrambled pieces meet your eyes and feel your pulse. For you know that in the pain, I feel your kingdom most. My Abba Daddy, healer and holder of my grief, you take it away and leave my lungs to breathe a sigh of peace. My King and my forever, my Lord, heals all in His time."

Amen, Jesus!

CHAPTER 14

The Power of Prayer

*He knows the way I take: when he has tested
me, I shall come forth as gold.*
—Job 23:10

The dictionary defines *prayer* as "a solemn request for help or expression of thanks addressed to God or to an object of worship." Although that is a narrow explanation, it is a place to start. From a very early age, I have been taught to pray. My parents prayed, my mom helped me say my night prayers, we prayed when we passed the church, we prayed when we heard an ambulance, we went to Mass every Sunday as a family, and we prayed in school. In elementary school I attended Mass every day; in high school and college, I studied religion. So I felt I had a solid footing when it came to prayer.

But *nothing* prepared me for the kind of praying that I would encounter when I became ill, was in a coma, and woke with no sense of where I was or what was going on. As I said before, all I had was GOD—just me and GOD. I had no speech, no breathing alone, no movement, no eating or drinking, *nothing*. My whole world was my thoughts and my heart, and the only one there beside me was GOD.

It was sort of like being in a pitch-dark forest. Have you ever seen true pitch blackness? No lights at all from the city or anywhere?

You struggle for your eyes to see, to focus on anything because of the darkness. Well that is what I experienced as I awoke from my coma—a vast nothingness. I could see people (barely), but I could not communicate at all, and I could not move at all. They were talking at me, and I could not respond in any way. It was just me and God. God had become personal in a whole new way. I mentioned earlier in this book that I felt at times like I was drowning in a raging sea and Jesus was holding out a branch for me to hang onto. As long as I hung on, I would not drown. But if I let go, I would be lost. I never thought of letting go of Jesus and his promises.

So I started a conversation (in my mind) like I never had before. My mind cried out to Him. I asked God to show me what I had done wrong in my life—and there was plenty! I had a long flashback of ways that I had failed God, and I had a chance to ask forgiveness. I asked Him to please help me heal for the sake of my family. I thanked Him for saving my life. I asked Him not to leave me alone. And I asked Him to lead me in His will daily.

Prayer became the solid foundation of my relationship with Jesus as I recovered from the coma and then went on to the rehab hospitals and then home where my journey of recovery continued. God was very kind to me and showed me many things throughout my recovery period. As I struggled with overwhelming grief, sorrow, loss, and fear, He was a gentle reminder in my heart that I would survive and He was always there.

I will never say that the road to recovery was easy. There was pain, frustration, doubt, fear, despair, loss, regret, unhappiness, even anger. In recovery, you experience a roller coaster of emotions throughout every day, and it is frightening. It is so important to recognize and accept the grief that goes along with such a traumatic and sudden event, and so much loss. It would be disrespectful to ignore the very human pain that we feel when we experience loss. Those feelings are *valid*, and we must acknowledge them in order to deal with them and move on in a healthy way.

My life changed forever in one day. My recovery was long and at times very painful physically and emotionally. *It* was the most difficult thing I have ever done in my life. I had to grieve—to walk through the pain of loss and change and not deny it. But the most important thing to know is *that I did not do it alone.* God was at my side through it all.

Prior to my illness, I enjoyed delving into many Christian books, and some were on prayer. When my daughter Jen left home in 2000 and I was distraught with fear, I began to pray intercessory prayers. These prayers pleaded with God for revelation and enlightenment for another person and for demolishing strongholds. I learned from many books and from my own spiritual walk that praying *God's word* is one of the most effective forms of prayer. In this way, God's words become alive within your own heart and mind. God tells us in the Bible *"So is my word that goes out from my mouth: It will not return to me empty, but will accomplish what I desire and achieve the purpose for which I sent it"* (Isa. 55:11).

One of the most joyful parts of my illness and recovery was the time I had to devote to prayer. In the stillness of the morning or at times throughout the night, I could meditate on what God was doing with me and saying to me. Prayer is not only asking; prayer is listening. Indeed, the ideal prayers have three parts—praising, petition, and listening. In other words, we start out thanking God for all He has done for us. Next we bring our prayer requests to him. We come boldly to the throne of grace! We specifically ask God for what we need while realizing He is the sovereign God and His will is central to our lives. So we lay our requests before Him, and then we wait in anticipation. I developed a strategy of doing this as I prayed almost nonstop in the rehab facility when I was alone. I would discuss what my feelings and fears were, then I would ask for something, and then

I told God I was waiting in anticipation. Most often, my requests were answered, but sometimes not in the way I expected! Listening is an important part of praying.

Although I haven't spoken much about the devil or Satan in this book, I need to acknowledge him as a very real, negative, evil force in the world. We know there is a God, and we must acknowledge that there is a devil. Satan has been called the father of lies, the author of confusion, the deceiving spirit, and he can masquerade as the angel of light. In other words, he is very deceptive and insidious. He can come to us through moments of despair, discouragement, and hopelessness. Those feelings can be reactions to grief, but when they become strongholds in our lives, we can suspect the work of the evil one. I struggled through some of these strongholds, and they are not pretty. Praying God's word at these times can keep our thoughts on track. It is always crucial to keep things in perspective. God is *bigger* than anything Satan can ever dream up, so you do not need to fear when you are a Christian! God is on your side always!

One day, as I was praying and talking to God about my discouragement, God led me to the passage about Jesus's temptation in the desert. Luke chapter 4 tells us that Jesus had gone to the desert to pray and fast. After forty days, He was hungry. The devil came to Him, knowing exactly where He was weakest at that time, and said "If you are the Son of God, tell this stone to become bread." Jesus replied, "It is written, man does not live by bread alone."

Again the devil showed Him the countryside and said, "Worship me, and all of this will be yours." Jesus said, "It is written, worship the Lord your God and serve Him only." The devil tries one more time. "If you are God, throw yourself down from here, for it is written… you will not strike your foot against a stone." Jesus replied, "It says, do not put the Lord your God to the test." The devil left Him.

I learned five things from this rich passage:

1. *Even Jesus was tempted.* Jesus was fully man and fully God at the same time. He suffered everything that we suffer as humans. He was spared nothing. He understood hunger, pain, fear, desire, loneliness, and He showed us how to deal with these things. The temptation of Jesus in the Bible is a model for us to follow and an encouragement to us in our difficult times.

2. *God allowed the temptation, and God allows the test.* Luke 4:1–4 says, *"Jesus full of the Holy Spirit returned from the Jordan and was led by the Spirit in the desert where for forty days he was tempted by the devil."* Wow! He was *led by the Spirit* to a place where God knew He would be tempted for forty days! Why? Because adversity is often a test. Adversity and temptation can reveal our weaknesses, so God can reveal His strength. In the desert, Jesus used the power of God's words and "it is written" to fight off the temptations of the devil. We can view our trials and adversity as tests that will reveal our weaknesses and ask God to show His power and strength, as Job did.

3. *The devil will tempt us at our weakest point, when we are suffering in some way.* Jesus was hungry and tired. He was also man, so I'm sure He would have loved to have some bread at that time. But he recognized that it was a trick of the devil, and He did not succumb.

4. *Jesus used God's own words as His weapon against the devil!* "It is written" means that it is already in the Holy Book, and once God has said something, it is a *fact*! It is *truth*. It is the way it is because God has said it. We must have the *faith* to believe that God's word is truth, and we will be able to fight off the fiery darts of the devil also.

5.   *The devil doesn't give up!* He came back at Jesus three times, but each time, Jesus fought him with the word of God. Finally, he stopped trying and left Jesus alone. You see, the devil knows God's word as well as—or better than—we do. And the devil knows that God's word, just like God, is all-powerful. So using God's word against the devil and at times of temptation is effective.

The phrase "it is written" is a powerful way to remind us that God's word is true. It can bolster our faith as we pray that phrase before each bible verse. For instance, Jeremiah 29:11 is one verse many people know. But to give it new meaning and a boost of power and faith in your heart, try this: "It is written that 'I know the plans I have for you, plans to prosper you and not harm you, plans to give you a future and a hope.'" Believe it in your heart of hearts, and ask God to increase your faith. We can increase our faith, which is a necessary ingredient to powerful praying. We should never pray simply for a religious activity. We must pray in faith, knowing that God's word is truth and will be effective. God tells us, *"The fervent (sincere) prayer of a righteous (faith-filled) man avails much"* (James 5:16).

The Bible is full of stories that God intends for us to use as a sort of model, or example, of the way He works in our lives, how He makes Himself and His principles known to us, and how He draws us closer to him continually. Stories such as the one about *Lazarus*, and how Jesus waited days before visiting his sick friend, then raised him from the dead to show the power of God; *Joseph*, the son of Jacob who was thrown into a well by his brothers who resented him, became a slave, endured suffering without losing hope, and who eventually became ruler of Egypt and took pity on his brothers; *Noah* who endured mockery but remained obedient to God's direction when building his ark, but then only he and his family were saved from the great flood; *David* the young boy who killed the giant Goliath with a slingshot; *Daniel* who was thrown into a lion's den but spared because of his faith in God; and so many more wonderful stories.

These are meant to bolster our faith, encourage our hearts, and provide a blueprint for how God's works in the lives of his children. When we feel discouraged, we can read these stories, identify with the suffering, and see how God rescued the faithful. In doing so, the Holy Spirit will quicken our hearts and minds to receive the message intended just for us. God cares for every detail of our lives!

When I first became ill and woke up paralyzed, I could no longer use the books I had collected on prayer. I could no longer read my Bible. I had God in my heart and mind, and no one could take that from me. But to bolster my faith, my family and nurses helped me to listen to my Christian praise music every night at bedtime with my iPhone and earbuds. I fell asleep praising God every night.

Later, after I was able to move my hands enough to use my phone, I put scripture verses in my phone, primarily on healing and miracles. You see, I was desperately asking God to heal me right away. At that time I couldn't understand what was taking so long and whether full healing would ever come! Just like when Jesus waited two days to visit Lazarus. Until after Lazarus had died, that was then Jesus could bring him back from the dead to show his glory. God often has a purpose in waiting. He was teaching me, leading me, showing me how to pray, how to turn to the Bible to increase my understanding and my faith, and preparing me to share my story and to witness to his mighty power. I also was able to store my prayer requests and praises in my phone.

Our journey on this earth is not just about us, in fact, it's not really about us at all. It is about the work God is doing for his kingdom and His plan for our lives and the lives of all His children. Every step along the way is the possibility of another seed planted as other people speak with us and observe our actions and our faith. *"Very truly I tell you, unless a kernel of wheat falls to the ground and dies, it remains only a single seed. But if it dies, it produces many seeds. Anyone who loves their life will lose it, while anyone who hates their life in this world will keep it for eternal life"* (John 12:24–25).

We have tremendous opportunities to encourage people every day, sometimes just through our actions. Every seed planted can be watered and nourished by God's love and grow into more people who know the good news. Rick Warren, author of *Purpose Driven Life*, starts his book by saying, "It's not about you." Although that is a hard concept to internalize, seeing our situation through the eyes of God's kingdom purposes gives us a new perspective. It can also give purpose to our pain. Romans 8:28 tells us, *"And we know that in all things God works for the good of those who love him, who have been called according to his purpose."* All things!

As my prayer life grew, my scripture verses grew. I prayed these verses every day and meditated on them. Sometimes certain words would literally jump off the page at me, and I knew God was speaking directly to my heart through His own mighty words. I know that is God's desire, and I pray the same will happen for you.

Telling this story was suggested to me by many people who encountered me along the journey—so many that it became an imperative for me to do this. As I mentioned earlier in the book, I felt that no one would be interested in me getting sick then getting better. God corrected me in an almost audible voice, saying, "It's not about you silly! It's about Me!" My deepest hope is that my account of this story has pointed often and totally to God! It clearly was not by my efforts that I was healed. Even doctors said it was a miracle that I was so suddenly and drastically ill, almost died, and then recovered completely. Only our amazing God can do such a thing.

As I compile these words and put the finishing touches on God's story, I am here in a magical, "almost paradise" environment that my dear friend allowed me to use to ensure that I have peace and quiet—a time away from everything, set aside to reflect on the majesty, glory, and power of our Almighty God in order to complete the writing of my story. My prayer is that God's power is evident and alive in each word, every story and through all the included scriptures. I am praying Isaiah 55:11, *"It will not return to me empty, but will accomplish what I desire, and achieve the purpose for which I sent it."*

God is full of surprises and affirmations if we open our eyes and hearts to look for them. After I arrived in the place where I would complete my story, I decided to attend church on Sunday morning. I found a nondenominational church ten minutes away and attended the early-morning service with great anticipation. The verse that way being handed out at the door by the greeters, which would be the basis of the message that morning, was the verse that brought me through my illness: *"Those who wait upon the Lord shall renew their strength; they shall mount up with wings like eagles; they shall run and not be weary, they shall walk and not faint"* (Isa. 40:31). God was affirming for me that I was in the right place and it was *time* to tell the story.

It just so happens that the location where I am writing is currently having a tropical storm—the first for this area in over ten years and certainly the first in my lifetime! I have been through lots of snowstorms, ice storms, hailstorms, and power outages, but never a tropical storm. Can you tell I come from the Midwest? I even like the sound of tropical storm much better—much warmer!

But what is utterly amazing to me as I peer out my window at the blowing trees and pouring rain and listen to the pounding thunder shaking the windows is the absolute *overwhelming power* of God! He is the Creator and Master of the universe. He is the one who has total control over nature—in its peacefulness or in its fury, such as I see raging outside right now. Why do we *ever* underestimate the power of the Lord who made heaven and earth? If He has the power to make the universe do whatever He wants it to, don't you think that He has the power to heal you? Do you believe?

I can thank God for the majesty of this awesome storm, and I have faith that the sun will come out once again. We don't know that for sure, but we have the faith to believe it! The laws of nature that we live by are only a promise! Why do we have trouble believing the promises of God? God's promises are true—you can believe that with all your heart and soul! What a blessing to me that God allowed me to be in a place such as this and experience His power in nature first hand, as I write His message for you. We serve an amazing God!

This tremendous tropical storm is something like my illness. It came on suddenly (yesterday was sunny and 90 degrees), it rages for a while and scares everyone and causes some damage, but then it passes. It moves on out to sea. It does not last forever. Another storm may come at some time, but God will be with us through that as well.

My illness did not last forever. I am healed and restored. Another illness may come at some time, but God will be with me through that as well. *That* is a promise you can believe in.

I have included the next chapter specifically because I wanted to make sure you have scriptures to pray and meditate upon as you seek God's grace and direction for your life. You cannot go wrong when praying scripture—it is the word of God and will not return empty. I pray these words reach your heart and spirit as they do mine.

The following chapter contains some of the most powerful verses under each topic listed. There are many more in the Bible, and I encourage you to discover more on your own. As I pray, there are times that I need to pray more in one category than another. For instance, if I feel I have unanswered prayers," I will concentrate on that section more than any others. Doing this often helps me to listen to what God wants me to know in my heart. God has equipped us to be overcomers, and using his word as our shield of faith will carry us forward. I pray that you will find the following scriptures to be as meaningful in your life as they are in mine. God bless you!

CHAPTER 15

Prayer Guide

Do not be anxious about anything, but in every situation, by prayer and petition, with thanksgiving, present your requests to God. And the peace of God, which transcends all understanding, will guard your hearts and minds in Christ Jesus.
—Philippians 4: 6, 7

Do you struggle with the concept of praying? We all have different backgrounds and experiences in this area. Some of us have no past experience praying, and others pray frequently and easily. Prayer is simply communication with God. God longs to hear your voice raised in prayer. His desire is constantly drawing us closer to Him. Faith is about a personal relationship with Jesus Christ. If you think of prayer as simple communication with a friend, it is not so daunting.

The most important decision of your life is to have a true, personal relationship with Jesus Christ. Anything else in your life pales in comparison. Giving your life to Jesus and accepting the free gift of salvation and His love is like having cancer and finding the cure! If you were ill and someone offered you a sure-fire cure, would you take it? You bet you would!

Without Jesus in our lives, we are all sick spiritually. We cannot be well without Him. This step is so important, so critical, yet so easy. We must believe and accept that fact that we are sinners. We are only saved by the grace of God. Then we must believe with our hearts that Jesus Christ died on the cross to save us from our sins. He became sin for us. Third, we must ask Him to come into our hearts, be our personal Savior, and commit our lives to following Him. If you have not yet done this, follow me in this prayer:

> *I admit, God, that I am a sinner and I need your grace and forgiveness. I believe that Jesus Christ died for me to pay the penalty for my sins and took my place on that cross. I am willing to turn right now from sin and accept Jesus Christ as my personal Lord and Savior. I ask you to send the Holy Spirit into my life to fill my heart and help me to become the kind of person you made me to be. Thank you, Jesus, for loving me. Amen.*

If you prayed that prayer along with me and gave your heart and soul to Jesus and accepted His free gift of salvation by His death on the cross, you are *saved*. You can be sure of that promise.

Romans 10:9 tells us, *"If you declare with your mouth 'Jesus is Lord,' and believe in your heart that God raised him from the dead, you will be saved."* Does this mean we will never sin again? Unfortunately not. We are human beings! Christ became human for our sake, to show us that we can overcome this world. Accepting Jesus Christ as your Lord and Savior means His grace will cover you and you will be assured salvation.

When we pray, we activate God's overwhelming, transformative power. We go to our Father in heaven, we thank Him for his blessings and his mercy, we tell our problems, we ask for help—then we wait for the answer. We watch our circumstances, and we ask for guidance every step of the way. We do not run ahead of God. We always seek God's will first—the right thing to say or do. God's got this! Remember, God has already won the battle. Always keep your eyes on Jesus! He knows your fear and pain and anxiety and wants you to trust Him.

When you pray, there are a few steps you can follow that will help prepare you for effective communication with our Lord and Savior. They don't have to be followed every time you pray, but they may prepare your heart for hearing His voice. Remember the three main steps are (1) thanksgiving, (2) petition, and (3) listening.

1. *Find a quiet time of day and a quiet place.* Early morning works best for me and for many others, but it certainly is not required. The Bible speaks of a "prayer closet," but any space that is set aside can be helpful. A comfortable chair, your Bible, a notepad and paper, and a dedicated time should do it.

2. *Come to God with an open heart.* Thank Him for his many blessings to you, and praise Him for His glory and might. Some people use the alphabet as a starting point, saying the letter and an attribute of God, such as "I praise you Lord for you are A, all-knowing, *B* benevolent, C caring; etc. After praising and thanking Him, let Him know that you want to be in the center of His will and you come before Him with an open heart and open hands.

   If you are struggling with unforgiveness or bitterness in your heart, ask God to help you handle that situation. He already knows everything about you, so bring it out into the open for healing. It is difficult to speak with God effectively if we are harboring such negative emotions. This will demonstrate your faith in God's healing power.

3. *State your petition.* Talk to Him about the situation troubling you. A disobedient child, a difficult boss, a troubled

marriage, an illness, financial problems, stress, fear, jealousy, envy, loneliness, pain, anger, rejection, heartache—the list goes on. Perhaps you need help in making a decision. We have many things to ask for, and God will listen to our pleas.

4. *Pray in the name of Jesus.* God delights when you honor his son. Praying "In the name of Jesus" is recognition of the power of God to do anything in His will.

5. *Listen to His voice.* After you have stated your thanksgiving, praises, and petitions, take time to be quiet and listen. Listening is part of any conversation, isn't it? Now it's your turn to listen. God speaks to us through the people and events in our lives, as well as the small, still voice in our heart. As you are listening, if God brings anything to your heart and mind, jot it down. A word, a phrase, a song, a memory, or perhaps an answer or directive. Did a Bible story suddenly jump into your mind? Jot it down, and record any thoughts and feelings you might be having. Be sure to date it, and keep it from day to day on your prayer walk with God.

6. *Pray in the will of God.* Whatever we are praying for must be in harmony with God's will for our life and the lives of others. For instance, we cannot pray for someone to get sick and die so we can take their job. We must pray within the righteousness also be faithful in prayer. Answered prayer comes to those who pray without ceasing. There is proper timing for answered prayer, and that timing is up to God. It doesn't mean that God is not listening or has not answered.

7. *Pray continually.* I cannot stress this enough. God's timing is not always our timing. I cannot stress this enough. I have had prayers answered immediately, in a little while,

and some not for years. When a long-standing prayer is answered, and you see how God's hand has creatively moved in response to your prayer, you will be in awe of the mighty God we serve. Don't ever give up! Do not be discouraged if you feel that you do not hear Him speaking right away. This takes practice. The more you apply this method, the easier it becomes.

Remember that God does not always answer prayers by filling your request right away. It is not a fast-food order line we're talking about—it is a relationship with the Creator of the universe! Also, keep in mind that God is sovereign—meaning He will do what He deems best in His almighty will. Part of getting to know God more is realizing that we must trust and surrender to His plans, knowing full well that He loves us and will never abandon us.

I spoke in the last chapter about spending time with God by praying His word. We know that "it is written," and because it is written, it is truth. If we accept this into our hearts and truly under-stand that His words are true, it will help our faith to grow. Once our faith grows, we will have the eyes and hearts to see God working all around us. I found the following scripture verses to be very helpful during my recovery period, and I pray and meditate on them to this day. I have memorized many of them and carry them in my heart.

They truly have become a "lamp to my feet and light to my path." When struggling with feelings that are overwhelming, and making it difficult to even know how to pray, read these verses slowly, one at a time. Let them soak into your heart. Let the Holy Spirit fill you with peace as you realize "it is written".

My suggestion is that you pray these scripture verses three times per day, claiming God's promises over you, your family, and your circumstances. God's word is true and never returns to Him empty. I hope you will find them helpful, and do the same.

When asking for healing

- "I can do all things through him who strengthens me." (Philippians 4:33)
- "And heal the sick that are with you and say unto them, the kingdom of God is come nigh unto you." (Luke 10:9)
- "Don't be afraid or dismayed. The presence of God will mend, repair, and heal every place you have been hurt! Let the Master Surgeon do what only He can do!" (Joshua 1:9)
- "God I am weak. Help me every day to put my trust in you. Help me to believe that you and I together can do anything." (Psalm 62)
- "For I will restore health unto thee, and I will heal thee of thy wounds said the Lord, because they called thee an outcast, saying the Lord will take from thee all sickness and will put none of the diseases of Egypt upon thee and will lay them upon those who hate thee." (Jeremiah 30:17)
- "Heal the sick, cleanse the lepers, raise the dead, cast out devils; freely ye has received, freely give." (Matthew 10:8)
- "But my God shall supply all your need according to his riches in glory by Christ Jesus." (Philippians 4:19).
- "And the prayer of faith shall save the sick and the Lord shall raise him up; and if he has committed sin, they shall be forgiven him." (James 5:15)
- "Now the God of hope fill you with all the joy and peace in believing, that you may abound in hope, through the power of the Holy Spirit." (Rom. 15:13)
- "Don't you know that you are God's temple and God's spirit lives in you?" (1 Cor. 3:16)
- "But they who wait on the Lord shall renew their strength; they shall mount up with wings like eagles; they shall run

and not be weary, they shall walk and not faint." (Isa. 40:31)

- "Oh Lord I called to you for help and you healed me." (Psalm 30:2)
- "'Jesus asked the man, 'What do you want me to do for you?' He replied, 'Lord I want to see.' Jesus said 'Receive your sight; your faith has healed you.'" (Luke 18: 35–43)

When praying for a miracle

- "Call to me and I will answer you and show you great and mighty things which you do not know." (Jeremiah 32:2–3)
- "I pray that the eyes of your heart may be enlightened in order that you may know the hope to which he has called you, the riches of his glorious inheritance in his holy people, and his incomparably great power for us who believe. That power is the same as the mighty strength he exerted when he raised Christ from the dead, and seated him at the right hand in the heavenly realms." (Ephesians 1:18–20)
- "I will lead the blind by ways they have not known, along unfamiliar paths I will guide them; I will turn the darkness into light before them, and make the rough places smooth. These are things I will do, I will not forsake them." (Isaiah 42:16)
- We rejoice in hope of the glory of God. Not only that, but we rejoice in our sufferings, knowing that suffering produces endurance, and endurance produces character, and character produces hope." (Romans 5:1–4)
- "So too the Holy Spirit comes to our aid and bears us up in our weakness: for we do not know what prayer to offer nor how to offer it worthily as we thought, but the Spirit himself goes to meet our supplication and pleads on our

behalf with unspeakable yearnings and groanings too deep for utterance." (Romans 8:26)

- "Tears are prayers too. They travel to God when we can't speak." (Psalm 56:8)
- "Praise the Lord O my soul and forget not all his benefits, who forgives all your since, heals all your diseases, who redeems your life from the pit and crowns you with glory." (Psalm 103:2–4)
- "The Lord will protect him and preserve his life, he will bless him in the land and not surrender him to the desires of his foes; the Lord will sustain him on his sickbed and restore him from his bed of illness." (Psalm 41:23)
- "Heal me O Lord and I will be healed. Save me and I will be saved, for you are the one I praise." (Jeremiah 17:14)
- "He said 'Daughter our faith has healed you. Go in peace and be freed from your suffering.'" (Mark 5:34)
- "You Lord give perfect peace to those who keep their purpose firm and put their trust in you." (Isaiah 26:3)
- "Arise! Shine! For your light has come, the glory of the Lord has dawned upon you." (Isaiah 60:1)
- "Ask and it shall be given to you; seek and ye shall find; knock and it shall be opened to you. For everyone that asks shall receive, he that seeks shall find, and to him that knocks it shall be opened." (Matthew 7:7–8)
- "Be joyful in hope, patient in affliction, faithful in prayer." (Romans 12:12)

When praying for hope

- "But thanks be to God! He gives us the victory through our Lord Jesus Christ!" (1 Corinthians 15:57)

- "Joshua said to them 'Do not be afraid! Do not be discouraged! Be strong and courageous. This is what the Lord will do to all the enemies you are going to fight!" (Joshua 10:25)
- "You will be secure, because there is hope, you will look about you and take your rest in safety. You will lie down, with no one to make ou afraid, and many will court your favor." (Job 11:18–19)
- "The Lord delights in those who fear hi, who put their hope in his unfailing love." (Psalm 147:11)
- "Hope deferred makes the heart sick, but a longing fulfilled is a tree of life." (Proverbs 13:12)
- "We also glory in our sufferings, because we know that suffering produces perseverance, perseverance character, and character, hope. And Hope does not put us to shame, because God's love has been poured out into our hearts through the Holy Spirit, who has been given to us." (Romans 5:3–5)
- "We rejoice in hope of the glory of God. Not only that, but we rejoice in our sufferings, knowing that suffering produces endurance, and endurance produces character, and character produces hope." (Romans 5:1–4)
- "You are my refuge and my shield; I have put my hope in your word." (Psalm 119:114)
- "Hope deferred make the heart sick, but a longing fulfilled is a tree of life." (Proverbs 13:12)

When praying for faith

- "Therefore I tell you, whatever you ask for in prayer, believe that you have received it, and it will be yours." (Mark 11:24)

- "Now faith is confidence in what we hope for and assurance about what we do not see." (Hebrews 11:1)
- "For we live by faith, not by sight." (2 Corinthians 5:7)
- "Because you know that the testing of your faith produces perseverance." (James 1:3)
- "Then Jesus declared, 'I am the bread of life. Whoever comes to me will never go hungry and whoever believes in me will never be thirsty.'" (John 6:35)
- "'Go,' said Jesus, 'your faith has healed you.' Immediately he received his sight and followed Jesus along the road." (Mark 10:52)

When struggling with fear

- "Say to those with fearful hearts, 'Be strong, do not fear, your God will come, he will come with vengeance, with diving retribution, he will come to save you.'" (Isaiah 35:4)
- "Peace I leave with you, my peace I give you, I do not give as the world gives. Do not let your hearts be troubled and do not be afraid." (John 14:27)
- "Have I not commanded you? Be strong and courageous. Do not be afraid, do not be discouraged, for the LORD your God will be with you wherever you go." (Joshua 1:9)
- "Therefore do not worry about tomorrow, for tomorrow will worry about itself. Each day has enough trouble of its own." (Matthew 6:34)
- "But now, this is what the LORD says—he who created you, Jacob, he who formed you, Israel "Do not fear, for I have redeemed you, I have summoned you by name. You are mine." (Isaiah 43:1).

- "Even though I walk through the darkest valley, I will fear no evil, for you are with me, our rod and your staff they comfort me." (Psalm 23:4)
- "I sought the LORD, and he answered me, he delivered me from all my fears." (Psalm 34:4)
- "When anxiety was great within me, your consolation brought me joy." (Psalm 94:19)
- "The LORD is my light and my salvation—whom shall I fear? The LORD is the stronghold of my life—of whom shall I be afraid?" (Psalm 27:1)
- "Cast all your anxiety upon him because he cares for you." (1 Peter 5:6–7)
- "For the Spirit God gave us does not make us timid, but gives us power, love, and self-discipline." (2 Timothy 1:7)

When struggling with grief

- "He will wipe every tear from their eyes. There will be no more death or mourning or crying or pain, for the old order of things has passed away." (Revelation 21:4)
- "The Lord is close to the brokenhearted and saves those who are crushed in spirit." (Psalm 34:18)
- "He heals the brokenhearted and binds up their wounds." (Psalm 147:3)
- "Blessed are the poor in spirit, for theirs is the kingdom of heaven." (Matthew 5:1–3)
- "And we know that in all things God works for the good of those who love him, who have been called according to his purpose." (Romans 8:28)
- "Blessed are they who mourn, for they shall be comforted." (Matthew 5:4)

When struggling with unanswered prayer

- "You do not have because you do not ask God." (James 4:2)
- "How long, O Lord will I call for help, and Thou will not hear?" (Habakkuk 1:2)
- "O my God, I cry by day, but Thou does not answer. And by night, but I have no rest." (Psalm 22:2)
- "If I regard wickedness in my heart, the Lord will not hear." (Psalm 66:18)
- "Your word is a lamp to my feet and a light to my path." (Psalm 119:105)

Be sure to search the Bible, and add more verses that you find of significance to you!

Appendices

These appendices are included to give you additional information on the topics discussed in the book, as well as references and resources to explore further. The information is as accurate as possible, but I am not a doctor—I was the patient! This is just a start. I encourage you to do further research for more information. Feel free to contact me by email if you wish additional information on anything I have discussed in the appendices.

* * * * *

Acute Respiratory Distress Syndrome

ARDS, or Acute Respiratory Distress Syndrome, is sometimes known as "wet lung." It is a life-threatening condition where fluid collects in the lungs' air sacs, or alveoli, blocking the organs of oxygen. ARDS is rather rare with fewer than 200,000 cases in the United States every year. ARDS can be caused by a direct or indirect injury to the lungs, such as a transplant, inhaling chemicals, trauma, septic shock, or aspirating vomit. This fluid buildup in the lungs causes the lungs to become stiff and heavy, and prevent the lungs from expanding as they should. The amount of oxygen circulating in the body can become dangerously low, even if on a ventilator. ARDS occurs along with failure of other organs, such as liver and kidneys.

The cause of ARDS is fluid leaked from the smallest blood vessels in the lungs into the tiny air sacs where blood is oxygenated. Normally a protective membrane keeps this fluid in the vessels. Severe illness or injury can cause inflammation that weakens this membrane leading to the fluid leakage of ARDS.

Symptoms develop quickly, in general within 24 hours of the illness or injury. Because they are so sick, people with ARDS often cannot talk about their symptoms. Typical symptoms are shortness of breath, rapid and difficult breathing, low blood pressure and organ failure. ARDS must be treated in an intensive care unit (ICU) and may involve medication to reduce fever, treat infections, stop inflammation, and remove fluid from the lungs.

A ventilator is used to deliver high doses of oxygen and positive pressure to the damaged lungs. People are often deeply sedated with medicines. Every effort is made to prevent further damage to the lungs. Treatment is mainly supportive until the lungs recover.

Estimates of mortality rates range from 30% to 90%, and often lung damage persists. The risk of death from ARDS goes us with age and severity of illness. While many people regain lung function, some are left with permanent damage. In addition, some are left with brain damage due to the time that oxygen was deprived from the brain.

(Information taken from the Mayo Clinic website at www.mayoclinic.org)

References:

- What is ARDS? *National Heart, Lung, and Blood Institute* http://www.nhibi.nih.gov/health/dci/Diseases/ards

- Post ARDS tips. *The ARDS Foundation*. http://www.ardusa.org/post-ards-tips
- AskMayoExpert. Acute respiratory distress syndrome. Rochester, Minn. Mayo Foundation for Medical Education and Research, 2014.

* * * * *

Vasculitis

According to the American College of Rheumatology, vasculitis is a term for a group of rare diseases that have in common inflammation of blood vessels. These vessels include arteries and veins. It causes changes in the walls of the blood vessels, including thickening, weakening, narrowing and scarring. These changes restrict blood flow, resulting in organ and tissue damage.

There are many types of vasculitis, and they vary greatly in symptoms, severity and duration. It can range from mild to life-threatening. It is rare with fewer than 200,000 cases in the US each year, and since the cause is unknown, it is incurable. Treatment may help. Early detection and treatment is the best option.

Vasculitis can result in poor blood flow to tissues throughout the body, such as the lungs, nerves, and skin. There are a wide range of signs and symptoms, including:

- Shortness of breath and/or cough, fever, headache, fatigue
- Numbness or weakness in hands or feet, loss of pulse in a limb
- Red spots on the skin, rash, night sweats, weight loss

Some types of vasculitis have no symptoms, such as that of the kidneys.

We don't know what causes vasculitis, but genetic factors may play a part. It is an autoimmune disease which means the body comes under attack by its own immune system. In vasculitis, the immune system attacks blood vessels.

The most common tests for vasculitis include biopsy, angiography, and blood tests. My doctors confirmed my diagnosis while I was in the medically induced coma by taking several biopsies of my kidneys. These were sent to the Mayo Clinic, and they confirmed microscopic polyangitis, or MPA. Most doctors detect the type of vasculitis by the size of the affected blood vessels and the organs affected. The most definitive test is for "antineutrophil cytoplasmic antibodies" or ANCA. A positive ANCA test can help detect Wegener's, microscopic polyangitis, or eosinophilic granulomatosis with polyangitis (Churg-Strauss).

The typical treatment for vasculitis includes steroids, such as Prednisone, and immune-suppressant drugs. Steroids reduce the inflammation but can have bad side effects. Doctors prescribe other types of drugs to prevent the use of steroids at times.

The strongest of the immune-suppressant drugs used is called cyclophosphamide, or Cytoxan. This is actually a chemotherapy drug and very effective with vasculitis, but typically not used for a long period of time due to side effects. Less serious vasculitis may be treated with methotrexate, azathioprine, or other immune-suppressant drugs. A newer drug called rituximab is very effective.

When my diagnosis of vasculitis was confirmed, I was prescribed 60 mg of Prednisone daily and 100 mg of Cytoxan. This continued from July 2014 until January 2015. While on Cytoxan, a strong chemotherapy drug, my hair fell out and my bladder was bleeding. I took Mesna to stop the bleeding. In January, I was still unable to move from the myopathy, but Cytoxan should only be taken for short periods of time. My rheumatologist studied blood tests and determined that we would try switching slowly to Imuran, which is azathioprine. Fortunately, I responded well to Imuran and still take 150 mg per day as a maintenance dose. We also started weaning very slowly from the Prednisone by 5 mg lower every two weeks. I currently take only 5 mg every other day and am doing well. God's grace carried me through the medication issues. I currently take sixteen types of pills every morning, only four of them over the counter, the rest prescription. Some are supplements such as magnesium and B12 to balance what the medications and illness do to the body. Praise God I have been well. I am having no side effects, and I pray daily that this will continue.

Vasculitis can be short term or lifelong, and doctors focus on preventing damage to organs. Some vasculitis patients suffer from fatigue, pain, arthritis, nose and sinus issues, and many other ailments.

Rheumatologists are the specialists who deal with vasculitis, but other specialist are often needed as well.

Resources for further reading:

- Suresh, E. *Diagnostic approach to patents with suspected vasculitis.*
- Internet: Diseases and Conditions Vasculitis—American College of Rheumatology
- Internet: *Mayo Clinic* - Vasculitis
- Internet: *WebMD* - Vasculitis
- Internet: National Institutes of Health
- Internet: www.medicineplus.gov
- Internet: www.hopkinsvasculitis.org
- Internet: www.vasculitisfoundation.org

* * * * *

Early Childhood Education

Early childhood education refers to early care and education of children from birth through third grade, with the main focus on the years prior to kindergarten. This time period is critical in a child's life because the most rapid and dramatic brain development occurs during this time. Experts say 80 percent of a young child's brain develops before kindergarten. Critical "windows" for development occur during which brains cells increase and thus become "hardwired" when they receive proper stimulation or die out as a result of lack of stimulation. For instance, the age of eighteen to thirty months is when a burst of language generally occurs. Toddlers this age often learn and speak four to ten new words per week. Their minds are primed for language development and act like sponges of the language they hear around them. Experts encourage lots of language opportunities and stimulation at this time such as reading books, singing, nursery rhymes, word games, and conversations. This is also a time period of intense emotional, social, and physical growth.

Many children at this age are cared for during the day in child care facilities in situations where parents or caregivers work and are unable to care for them during the day. It is essential that the child care workers are trained and that the facility is of very high-quality to ensure optimal development and learning. Different theories exist regarding the best way to teach and nurture our youngest children. One theory with which I have worked, trained on, and endorsed throughout my career is the Reggio Emilia Approach. As part of my professional role, I visited Reggio Emilia, Italy and studied the philosophy firsthand. This is a world-acclaimed philosophy that views children as capable and curious and fosters a sense of creativity, wonder, and exploration. Emergent curriculum is child-initiated and teacher-facilitated. Documentation of learning is posted for parents, children, and educators to see and revisit, encouraging further exploration. Important principles in this approach include the image of the child, the role of the teacher, project work, and the environment as the third teacher.

In the Reggio Emilia approach, the environment is considered an essential part of the learning experience. The Reggio educators consider it the third teacher, meaning it should be set up in such a way that the children can interact and learn from it without interruption from the teacher. Aesthetic beauty, nature, creativity, order, and authentic, stimulating materials create an environment of wonder and inspiration. Based on our experiences in utilizing this philosophy of teaching in the child care company where I was employed, the classroom environments in our centers were taken to a new and unique level. No other preschools or child care centers looked the way our centers did. We established principles of design, and several of us decided to collaborate on a book about environments entitled *"Inspiring Spaces for Young Children"* and a companion book called *"Rating Observation Scale for Inspiring Environments."* By utilizing solid design principles such as nature, color, focal point, etc., we transformed ordinary classrooms into places of beauty and wonder. These books have proven very popular with educators hoping to improve their classrooms. They are published by Gryphon House and are available on Amazon. I am one of the five authors and still offer trainings on the concepts.

During my career prior to my illness, I did a lot of training on various early childhood topics. The Inspiring Spaces books became a favorite for training opportunities which I enjoyed tremendously. After my illness and recovery, I have resumed consulting with other centers, training and working closely with other early childhood professionals. This is my passion, and God has granted me the privilege of continuing in it!

But what happens to those children who do not have the opportunity to learn in a high quality environment, or who don't have a chance to attend a child care center? Many children spend their early years at home, and that is fine if there is proper stimulation, such as reading books, going places, and lots of loving and nurturing. Some children, however, are in situations that are not nurturing and not stimulating. Some statistics say almost half of the children under five in the US live at or near poverty. This can be tragic because lack of stimulation, coupled with inadequate care, and the presence of stressful situations prevent children from developing properly. Constant stress causes the release of cortisol in the brain, which is the "fight or flight" response, and negatively affects development and causes a hypersensitivity of emotions. Many of these children come to kindergarten unable to learn, some of them 75 percent behind their middle-class peers.

Programs are in place to help these disadvantaged children. Many states have subsidies which allow low-income parents who are working or going to school to pay only a small portion of high quality care while the state subsidized the rest. Although expensive, this program is essential for the purpose of educating our youngest citizens and preparing them to enter Kindergarten ready to learn. The positive impact of high quality child care for disadvantaged children is well known. High quality preschool can be linked to higher high school graduation rates, lower need for special education, lower incarceration rates, and higher rates of employment as adults.

After my illness and recovery, I began to do work for an organization called Ohio Association of Child Care Providers. OACCP is a group of volunteer child care owners, directors, and professionals who work together to speak with one voice to advocate for early childhood education, inform legislators about issues, and impact state decisions regarding subsidized child care. This is critically important work and our organization strives to ensure that adequate funding is available for quality programs.

As executive director, I became the face of OACCP. Working primarily from home, I grow membership, speak at meetings, communicate with members regularly, and help with advocacy work. I enjoy working in my chosen field with other administrators and owners, and love the challenge of interacting with state government officials. Mostly, I love advancing the cause of supporting high quality early care and education.

In addition, I do some grant-writing with a local organization called Baby University, which is a parenting class for underprivileged and very young parents in South Toledo, teaching them how to nurture, discipline, and teach their young children. This has truly been a gift in my recovery period and continues today.

References:

Edwards, C., Gandini, L. & Forman, G. (1998) The hundred languages of children—Advanced reflections (2nd edition) Greenwich, CT. Ablex

Heckman, James J. The Economics of Inequality" American Educator Magazine, Spring 2011. Pgs. 31-47.

Inspiring Spaces for Young Children. Jessica DeViney, Sandra Duncan, Mary Ann Rody, Sara Harris, Lois Rosenberry. Gryphon House. Silver Spring Md 201

Rating Observation Scale for Inspiring Environments. Jessica DeViney, Sandra Duncan, Mary Ann Rody, Sara Harris, Lois Rosenberry. Gryphon House 2010

About the Author

Mary Ann Rody served as chief operating officer of a local child care chain with nine centers, over 200 staff members and 1,700 children. Her tenure of twenty-six years included earlier positions as kindergarten teacher, administrator, human resource manager, and vice president. In addition to her work, Rody coauthored the books entitled *Inspiring Space for Young Children* and *Rating Observation Scale for Inspiring Environments*. She has presented at conferences locally and nationally and served on various professional boards. Rody has a BA in Psychology from John Carroll University in Cleveland, Ohio, and has nearly completed her master's in early childhood Education. Rody is married with three adult children and lives in Ohio where she now serves as executive director of a state association of child care providers in addition to doing consulting work and grant-writing for a local nonprofit charity. She and her husband currently attend a nondenominational church in their area.

CPSIA information can be obtained
at www.ICGtesting.com
Printed in the USA
LVOW06s1259110517
534153LV00024B/507/P